Nostradamus
His Key to the Centuries

[signature]

09/11/ 1995

V. J. HEWITT

NOSTRADAMUS

HIS KEY TO THE
CENTURIES

PROPHECIES OF BRITAIN
AND THE WORLD
1995-2010

BCA

LONDON   NEW YORK   SYDNEY   TORONTO

This edition published by BCA by arrangement
with William Heinemann Ltd
an imprint of Reed Consumer Books Ltd

Copyright © V. J. Hewitt 1994
The moral right of the author has been asserted
Reprinted 1995

CN 5821

Typeset by Falcon Graphic Art Ltd
Wallington, Surrey
Printed and bound in China
Produced by Mandarin Offset

C O N T E N T S

Nostradamus
His Key to the Centuries

Portrait véritable et remarquable du fameux Michel Nostradamus astrologue célébre.

L.4.

J'annonce vérité simplement et sans pompe.

Et mon présage vrai nullement ne me trompe.

Michel Nostradamus naquit à S.t Remy petite Ville de provence le 14 decembre de l'an 1503 à l'heure de midi il était fils de 3 jacques.
Nostradamus notaire Royal de cette Ville et de Renée de S.t Remy damoiselle, il était petit fils tant paternel que maternel de médecins et mathématiciens célébres il fut reçu docteur en l'université de Montpellier dont il exerça la charge de professeur, ce grand homme a vécu sous les regnes de Louis XII, François I.er Henry II. et Charles IX dont il fut médecin, il retourna à Salon autre Ville de Provence et y mourut en bon chrétien après avoir été tourmenté par les goutes qui dégénérées en hydropisie, le suffoquèrent au bout de huit jours ayant prédit l'heure et le jour de sa mort, qui arriva entre trois et quatre heures du matin le 2 juillet 1566.

A Paris chez Jean Rue S.t Jean de Beauvais N.o 10.

Nostradamus, early nineteenth-century engraving

Montpellier, sixteenth-century town plan

2

INTRODUCTION

Nostradamus

MICHEL de Nostredame — Nostradamus — was born in Provence on 14 December 1503 by the Julian calendar. His family was Jewish, converted to Roman Catholicism. He attended the University of Avignon and then gained a degree from the leading medical school at Montpellier.

After some years in independent practice, he returned in 1529 to Montpellier to take his doctorate and remained there as a lecturer until 1531, when he moved to Agen, married and renewed his practice.

Die Statt Montpellier mit jhrer gelegenheit.

Erklerung etlicher örter dieser Statt.

A Zu unser Frawen.
B Die Thi.
C S.Firmin.
D S.Peters Gestifft/Bischoffs Sitz.
E Der pallast.
F S.Hilari.
G Das Prediger Closter.

H Der Weg von Hignas,
I Der Weg gen Pezenas/
K Der Wahl.
L S.Guilheims Gassen.
M Die Nonnen von S.Guilhelm.
N Zu S.Magdalena.
O Ein Straß zu einem ort Charnis genannt.

P Die kleine Observantz.
Q S.Thoman.
S S.Sauuatre.
T Die Straß von Besolers.
V Der groß S.Johanns.
X Die groß Observantz.

Y Der Weg gen Lates.
Z Der Weg zu der Bruck Juuencau.
aa Saltzhaus.
bb Die inner Statt.
cc Fischmarckt.
dd Das Richthauß.
ee S.Denys.

D ij   Von der

3

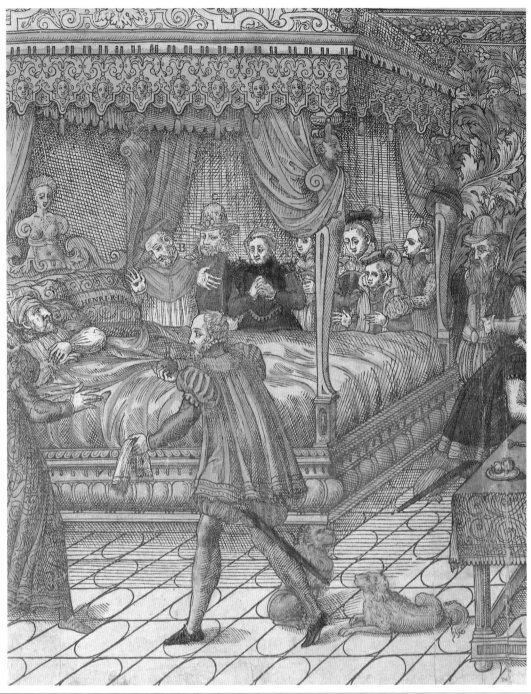

The death of
Henri II,
which
Nostradamus
predicted

A few years later his wife and two young children died from plague and Michel, racked by grief and the focus of attention by the Inquisition (throughout his life he was troubled by investigations of alleged heretical and sorcerous practices), left France to wander through Europe. In 1547, having returned to Provence, he married again and settled at Salon where he wrote several books, including a compendium of home recipes for medicines, cosmetics and love-potions. In 1550, he began publishing a series of almanacs and in 1555, his first collection of long-term prophecies appeared under the title *Siècles*, or 'Centuries'.

A year later he was summoned to the French Court in Paris by the Queen, Catherine de Medici, to interpret one of his prophecies which seemed to hint at blindness and death threatening the King, Henry II. Catherine had already been warned of a similar fate for Henry by an Italian astrologer. In Paris, Nostradamus warned Catherine and Henry of danger threatening the King from any form of single combat.

On 28 June 1559, three years after Nostradamus had returned home, Henry was wounded in one eye while jousting with the captain of his Scottish guard. Henry died ten days later. The prophecy was quoted in the city, riots broke out and calls were made for the Church to intervene, but Nostradamus remained untroubled in Provence (in those days a month's journey from the capital). He published no more prophecies during his lifetime. In 1564, Catherine visited him at Salon with her young son, Charles IX (her first son, Francis II, had died of illness in 1560, eighteen months after his father, an event also predicted by Nostradamus).

Nostradamus died in 1566.

In 1568, a larger collection of 942 prophecies appeared in the form known today. They were written as quatrains, four-line verses of alternate rhyming couplets, and divided into sections of 100 prophecies each, except for the seventh section, or 'century', which contains only 42.

CHAPTER 1:
ENIGMA AND PROMISE

ON 4 August 1981, I detected the first evidence that the prophecies of Nostradamus, the sixteenth century French physician and seer, had been written in a code possessing logical and consistent rules by which it could be deciphered.

Compared with what I have since learned, that evidence was minute – contained in a single word – but at the time the discovery appeared to be momentous. From my limited knowledge of the history of the prophecies I instinctively felt that it was unprecedented. No one had ever extracted this information before.

It is difficult to explain my feelings at that moment. I experienced a kind of delighted recognition as if I already knew, on that sunny August morning, that the discovery was intended for me alone. It is an odd sensation, being at the focal point of past, present and future. I have since experienced it many times when decoding his text; like something clicking, not only inside your head, but also out there in the exterior world, a distorted balance being adjusted, as if we were meant to perceive life in this way all along, but have simply forgotten how to.

I also sensed that this discovery was only the beginning. It's fortunate that I personally cannot see into the future! Had I known just how many years of intense research lay ahead – five to understand the text, two to establish some ground rules about the dating system and another two to begin extracting predictions of the future, I might have given up. Although I believe not. Fascination is still as strong as ever.

But, on that day in 1981, I had no knowledge of all this.I was standing at the beginning of a path that led into the very heart of the prophecies – a hitherto unknown path, I reasoned. If someone else had glimpsed the way in, it would surely be public knowledge.

However, as the months went by and I made increasingly significant discoveries, I began to ask questions.

Using the method of detection I had discovered, I had already been able to dissect item after item of information about historical events concealed within each prophecy — information framed in sensible prose, not incoherent verse, clear, precise and, above all, *accurate*. (Nostradamus died in 1566. To him all references to events after that date are predictions, whereas to me all prophecies relating to events prior to 1981, the date of my discovery, were prophecies of the past, an invaluable research ground for comparing newly discovered predictions in the text with recorded historical fact.)

How was it that I, who had no relevant background, was extracting such material? One answer was: 'why not me?', but I did begin to wonder if the ground *had* already been covered by another of the many students of Nostradamus since his death in 1566. Perhaps someone else had gone down the same path, made the same calculations, found that they contained errors and discarded this approach that to me seemed to promise so much. Perhaps everyone who had ever written about Nostradamus knew about this 'false' entrance. I began to collect commentaries on his prophecies and read them one after another, attempting to detect any reference that might suggest I was following the work of someone else.

It was then that I made an extraordinary discovery.

When I read these other commentaries on Nostradamus, old or modern, they all seemed to be speaking a different language from the one I had established to understand his work. Nothing I read made any sense and yet these were all respected scholars who had contributed immensely to the knowledge of Nostradamus and the interpretation of his prophecies. I can only say what I felt. I could not get to grips with anything they said. I looked at my own work and compared it to theirs. I could find no common ground, no familiar points of reference. In the space of a few months, the path I had chosen to follow had taken me so far away from anyone else doing the same work that I could no longer make any

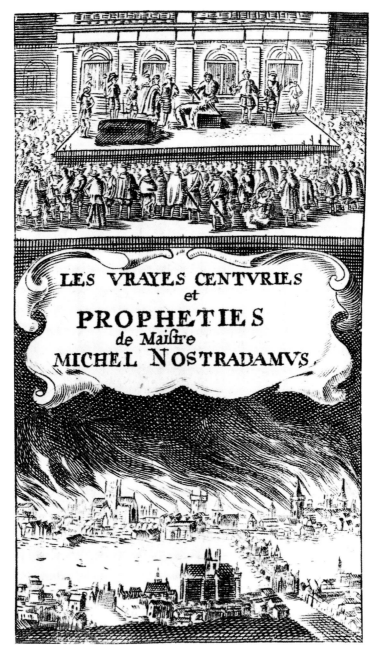

A seventeenth-century edition of Nostradamus's *Centuries,* illustrating the fire of London

connections with what the other commentators were saying.

True, I would sometimes agree with another writer that a prophecy might refer to a particular event in history, say, the French Revolution, but always I would be searching for an underlying consistency, an analytical method that would tell me without any doubt that the verse was referring to the French Revolution and to nothing else.

It meant locating names, personal and place, clear, accurate references and, ultimately, a dating system. The method would have to be the same wherever I applied it to any single prophecy. Nowhere could I find traces from any other trail except my own over the ground that I was uncovering.

I was either stupendously wrong – or right.

Fortunately, by comparing prophecies of past events with recorded historical information I was receiving repeated confirmation that I *was* right. When I applied the decoding system, the accuracy of the prophecies was breathtaking.

In trying to understand each prophecy there had always been one point where my interest diverged sharply from other commentators. Whereas they were always trying to understand the meaning of the distorted prophecy, *I was becoming fascinated by its physical appearance on the page and the way each verse seemed to have been 'constructed', rather than just written.*

The prophecies of Nostradamus are notoriously difficult to read – intentionally so. Nostradamus himself wrote that he had deliberately 'twisted' the original prophecies into the obscure form by which they are known today. Anyone who has attempted to read his work will agree that he did a sound job. The syntax is muddled, the style and sense is intensely compressed ('telegrammese' one of his biographers, James Laver, called it) as if the seer were writing press headlines. And then, as if these problems were not enough, there is the atrocious spelling.

Printing was an infant technology in the sixteenth century and standard forms of spelling still had to emerge. Even so, the spelling in the prophecies often bears little relationship to the *sound* of the word being spelt. When I took in this point, I had realised something very important.

Exotic spellings occur often in the prophecies – and Nostradamus wrote nearly a thousand in *Siècles*, the collection that we know today.

What form do these distortions take? Here, everything becomes very odd, because the spellings bear hardly any relationship to what they should have been. Misspelling on the part of a writer either indicates carelessness, the occasional letter left out or put in the wrong place, or, if the habit is deep-seated, it reflects a chronic inability to spell.

Where the writer finds difficulty in spelling, he tries to follow the *sound* of the word. He tries to spell it phonetically. In the attempt to follow the sound he leaves out extraneous letters, especially those not included in the sound of the word, for he does not think of them as being there. He does not:

a   insert many more letters
b   chop off whole syllables, especially when they contain part of the *sound* of the word he is trying to spell.

Yet these two activities are precisely what we encounter in the prophecies of Nostradamus. Either a word has letters that cannot conceivably belong there, or whole syllables are missing even when they carry a vital part of the sound of the word.

The excuse that it might have been the fault of the printer simply does not wash. In the sixteenth century, time was money to a printer as it is now. If he had produced a proof so dramatically different from the original he would not have been paid.

There can be only one answer. Nostradamus himself deliberately inserted letters into his lines of text because it was necessary that they should be there. He deleted other, apparently essential letters because it was necessary that they should *not* be there.

Why did he perform this dual action? *It could only have been because the letters themselves, irrespective of the apparent subject of the distorted prophecy, were the key to understanding the underlying system which links all of the prophecies.*

When I realised this, the penny finally dropped. At that moment I realised that one had only to cease thinking of Nostradamus' verses as muddled prophecies, to start thinking of them as carefully assembled collections of letters. Once you know that, you know the way into the prophecies.

If the verses must be regarded only as collections of letters, how should the interpreter proceed? What redeems these so-called prophecies from becoming nonsense? Only a thinly-drawn line between muddle and the sudden emergence of vivid, accurate details which seem to describe an historical event.

Take, for example, the famous prophetic verse:

i

Le sang de juste à Londres fera faute,
Bruslez par foudres de vingt trois les six,
La dame antique cherra de place haute,
De mesme secte plusieurs seront occisr.

II.51

Roughly translated, the meaning appears to be:

"The blood of the legitimate one will be faulted by London, you burn by unexpected events of twenty three six, the ancient lady will fall from her high place, of the same sect many more will be in the west."

What does this odd verse mean? For a hundred years after Nostradamus' death in 1566, it would have meant nothing at all. Only the word 'London' would have suggested that the prophecy was connected with England. Then in 1666, the Great Fire of London broke out. It began at a baker's shop in Pudding Lane and destroyed much of the city, including St Paul's Cathedral and many Protestant churches.

Suddenly the prophecy takes on meaning.

The 'legitimate one' can be identified as Charles I, executed in 1649, while the year when the 'unexpected' fire destroyed

London was 1666 (twenty times three plus six equals sixty-six.) The 'ancient lady' is more difficult, but 'she' can be construed as St Paul's Cathedral if we remember the tradition that it was built on a former Roman temple of Diana. The goddess was known in Europe and Britain as 'the lady' or 'the dame' up until only a couple of centuries ago.

Nevertheless, it can be argued (and it always is) that, although some of the detail in the verse is striking, the verse does not convey the certainty that this is a prophecy about the Great Fire of London, or indeed about *any* event at all. The spelling is wrong, the syntax is muddled, and there are no hard facts such as names, places, or dates – with the exception of 'London'.

In previous books I have argued that Nostradamus wrote his prophecies in long, imprecise anagrams. The solutions of these anagrams use up all the letters in the original prophecy, but substitute one letter per word, if necessary.

How does the recognition of this system affect the 'Great Fire of London' prophecy?

i

Le sang de juste à Londres fera faute,
Bruslez par foudres de vingt trois les six,
La dame antique cherra de place haute,
De mesme secte plusieurs seront occisr.

Perceiving the first two lines as a single anagram, followed by another anagram in the last two lines, what emerges is:

g   *j*
Après la peste fuit, le feu rase Londres,
     d   *z*   *d*   *d*   *g*
Brulé vite par les fours, l'an soixante six.
      q   *e*   *m*   *t*
L'huche à pain cuit à la cathédrale de Saint Paul,
o   *o*   *c*   *c*
Les erreurs du Messie semées.

> After the plague flees, fire razes London,
> swiftly burned through ovens, the year sixty-six,
> The bread bin cooks St Paul's Cathedral,
> The errors of the Messiah scattered."

The letters above the text are 'old' letters from prophecy II.51. The letters immediately below them are 'new' or inserted letters. Both sets of letters justify their place by joining to form the dating system (see 'Understanding the Code').

The combination of details presented by this new prediction is now such that it cannot possibly be describing any other event. Remember, the Fire occurred one hundred years after the death of Nostradamus.

References to 'ovens' and a 'bread bin' pinpoint the Fire's origin at a baker's premises in Pudding Lane. These phrases are not intended to conjure up childish pictures, but the kind of 'cartoon imagery' we see in the press today, using incongruous details to drive home a point.

It has been suggested that Nostradamus was a secret Protestant, despite his family's 'conversion' to Roman Catholicism at a time when to have remained in the Jewish faith would have meant exile from France. Judging from the last line, it would seem that he was stating a Jewish view of Christianity as an heretical offshoot of Judaism.

After my initial discovery in 1981, I had, through constant experiment, reached this stage of understanding the prophecies by about 1983. The next stage lay several years away, but marked a quantum leap in terms of the advance it represented.

So far, we have seen that Prophecy II.51 is capable of yielding up information about the Great Fire of London that no one has ever known was there.

The second stage is the realisation that, by using the letters in the prophecy in different combinations, breaking them down and building them up again into different words about different subjects, it is also capable of predicting other events which have nothing to do with the Great Fire of London. For instance:

ƒ   *x*   *d*

Cinq: l'économie de la Grande Bretagne, il la faut juste

p   *h*   *d*   *p*   *s*   *r*

évaluation. Au lieu de cela, vous rusez à surestimer hausse en

     s   *r*   *s*

dépreciations. Sert à mesestimer déficit.

"1995 onwards — the economy of Great Britain needs a fair assessment. Instead, you deceive by overestimating the rise in depreciations. It serves to underestimate the deficit."

This is one of the predictions in this book, also decoded from Prophecy II.51 (see 'Deception in the British Economy'). The use of the time word *cinq* has 'told' the original prophecy to predict the state of the British economy from 1995 onwards. Here, Nostradamus has issued a stern warning to the governments of the day.

For predictions on subjects relating to 2000 onwards, I use a different time phrase.

So this second vital stage consists of choosing a subject, putting it through the decoding process by drawing out the letters of that subject from the prophecy — and what remains of the verse is an anagram of a corresponding prediction.

What's more, the dating system will automatically follow your subject.

So if you want to know what the prophecies have to say about Margaret Thatcher, trends in leisure, the British Royals, or the future of the South American rain forests, you can find out by using this process. In fact, predictions on all four subjects appear in this book. The dates will follow. And you can use any prophecy to do it. The collections of letters in each prophecy vary in type and frequency, so no prediction will ever be quite the same. But no prediction will contradict another one. In two predictions about the same subject, two different aspects of that subject will be highlighted, or further information will be offered which draws in a second subject.

What would you like to know about the future? How will environmental pollution affect us in years to come? What's the weather going to be like for Venusian colonists? Do the nations of the European continent at last get their act together? All of these questions and more are answered in the following pages.

The process is not easy. It has taken me twelve years to get this far. Before I reached the point of being able to extract predictions of the future I had spent years studying hundreds of texts predicting events of the past, and made tens of thousands of calculations. I had discovered in myself a capacity for concentrating on a single line of text for hours at a stretch. Every so often a line of verse would suddenly blur momentarily in front of my eyes. I would realise that its syllables could be transposed to make up a completely different sentence, one with precisely spelt names and detailed predictions – nothing that had ever been seen before in connection with Nostradamus, or, indeed, with any form of prophecy that we know.

As the years went by I learned the basic rules of decoding the text, how to begin implementing the dating system – and finally, this Great Secret, that any of the hundreds of prophecies published by Nostradamus were capable of predicting on more than one subject. In fact, they were capable of prophesying on *any* subject, far into our own future.

I was once asked why, if any single prophecy could do the job, Nostradamus wrote so many. At first I was stumped for an answer, but then I realised that he had written them with the object of enabling as many single prophecies as possible to survive. It is the *massive* amount of his prophecy which fascinates people, just as much as their content. Whole lifetimes have been spent combing through the hundreds of prophecies. Any one prophecy would not have survived. A great work of nearly a thousand came to be treated with much more respect.

However, the main reason for so many prophecies is that the number, type and frequency of letters in each quatrain has a direct relationship with the information that emerges. Two different 'generative' prophecies will echo the same trend, predict the same events, but because of the separate makeup of their letters, each one will highlight different aspects. With such a device, a map of the future, with each new prediction as a reference point, gradually emerges.

When I realised that each and every prophecy was capable of performing this task, I had made the breakthrough. That it took ten years for me to reach it may now appear extraordinary, but I think more than anything it was my own reluctance to accept the implications of what I was achieving which held me back. I had to be sure, with each tentative step I took into the unknown, that I had evidence convincing me I was right.

I often have to talk or give interviews about my work and the usual reaction is a healthy scepticism, and sometimes open hostility, not to the idea of being able to catch glimpses of the future (most people have experienced those to some degree), but to the extraordinary precision and detail of the predictions which emerge using the decoding system. 'Nostradamus couldn't have known about this politician or that film star', they say, or 'how could he have known about computers, or television, or space travel?'

A few years ago, I would have argued that, of course, he knew all about the predictions emerging from the system that I was using. Now I am not so sure. My answer would probably be: 'Yes, he could know about all these things if he wanted to – but why would he want to?'

A French Jew of the sixteenth century would want to learn about the fate of Protestantism which had risen in his own lifetime, the destiny of France and the fate of Jews throughout Europe.

I am a woman of *my* time. I want to know how ecological pollution will affect society over the next century, whether the divide between rich and poor will be resolved, where society is going and what are the technological developments we can expect over the next century.

A person in 2094 will, again, have a different list of priorities.

So what if Nostradamus devised, not a 'hands-on' operation, one in which he was personally involved in speaking through every prediction, but a 'hands-off' one, in which he constructed this system to float free through the centuries? It is a staggering thought and one which will take a great deal of getting used to.

The main aspect of the system – the transmutation of letters and numbers – is, I believe, directly related through Nostradamus to the Jewish Kabbala, a mystical tradition of prophecy using the 22 sacred letters of Hebrew. Schools of Kabbalistic learning flourished in medieval times, but the Kabbala's roots stretch back to Ancient Egypt. Although much of the teaching was oral and has therefore remained secret, one of its main principles was the transposing of letters in a word to make other words – the application of the anagram. The language of Hebrew is suited to such techniques. So is French, although the Nostradamus alphabet consists of 24 letters, two more than in Hebrew. The thirteenth century teacher of the Kabbala, Rabbi Abraham Abulafia, taught that any language, not only Hebrew, could become the vehicle of prophecy by reordering these sacred letters in certain specified ways.

In these prophecies, we see the master creation of Nostradamus adapted from these ancient teachings and based upon the French language, which 'teaches' the determined pupil how to detect predictions within the prophecies. With years of practice, the two halves of the brain, the mathematical time-telling left brain and the timeless right brain (which can see past, present and future as a single unity, but cannot articulate it) come together in a joint exercise. (This 'joining' has a physical effect. After several hours of concentrated decoding, although the skull seems the same size, the mind feels as if it has been stretched out along a horizon ending two or three feet on either side of the body. It can take upwards of an hour for it to 'shrink' back inside the head, but while this happens you feel intensely alert.)

With this reasoning, the total sum of Nostradamus' prophecies becomes a great, independent construction which people of each generation, with time and patience, can learn to use. Their massive bulk can be compared to a machine built centuries ago, but with the key to its working lost. Over the years many people have tried to guess what its function was, or how the different parts worked, but a consistent theory has never emerged. Now, by pulling a few levers, or pressing some buttons in different sequences, a section of the machine has suddenly purred into life. Many of its parts remain silent, however, and the underlying principles governing its activity have yet to be established in full. What else, I wonder, will emerge? Only time will tell.

So when I am asked if he knew every detail of these new predictions, I reply: 'I don't know.' I *do* know that the prophetic material which he left is capable, using the system I have discovered, of producing predictions containing detailed and accurate forecasts of our future.

Nevertheless, in order to construct this 'machine', he must always have possessed an immense overview of the future, springing from natural prophetic talent. Therefore, whenever I interpret what a prediction is saying, I always refer to Nostradamus. After all, who can tell whether or not that magician of language is standing nearby and overseeing the continuation of his work?

Certainly, he has not been left behind in past centuries. He walks with us as we journey into what was once unknown, but is no longer so. At the junction of the ages, we should pause to hail his marvellous achievement, for, in this weird dimension called time, it will not be long before we meet again.

In the mists of the future, our guide is waiting.

CHAPTER 2:

PLANET EARTH 1995–2010

OUR world is speeding towards a new century, a new millennium, a new astrological age – the age of Aquarius, whose symbol is that of a human figure, sometimes man, sometimes woman, pouring a libation of water onto the thirsty ground. In this coming era, the care of our homeland planet will become our overriding concern as we begin to repair the destruction caused by the old industrial age, vanished for ever in a welter of strange, eco-friendly sciences and technologies.

Sign of Aquarius from the Bedford House. Under this sign Nostradamus predicts changes in every corner of the globe

Normandy – dukedom of William the Conqueror

However, that is looking far into the future. What we, in this dying decade, have to face is the 'turbulence' created by the imminent birth of these three times.

At the beginning of this century, Britain was a superpower controlling a quarter of the planet. China and Russia were ruled by emperors and tsars. America had turned from exploring a continent to a fascination for technology. Europe was a polyglot of tense and complex alliances endeavouring to compete with the rising power of a German state born only decades before. World wars, space travel, incredible advances in medicine, undreamed-of leisure and famines that killed millions still lay in the future.

A *thousand* years ago, William of Normandy, the conqueror of England and the shaper of a nation's destiny, was not yet born. Saxon kings had ruled England for six centuries. Britain and Europe were governed by systems formed after the fall of imperial Rome in the fifth century. European paganism was engaged in a desperate, centuries-long battle with a newly militant Church. Nearly five centuries before Columbus, Viking explorers had established ocean-wide links with the red race inhabiting a continent that would one day be called 'America'. Travellers of the Silk Road, trading routes linking China with Europe, brought back fabulous tales of mythical beasts and men. Byzantium, second capital of the Roman emperors, still stood guard against the East.

2500 years ago, the astrological age of Pisces was just beginning. Its main features have been the spread of ideas from Confucius to Marx, the rise of new world religions, Buddhism, Christianity and Islam, urbanisation as people left the fields and woods and moved into great cities, and, finally, the coming of advanced technology.

Pisces represents the breaking of essential links between the hunter/farmer and the electronic wizard. Not for nothing is the sign of Pisces two fishes, one swimming upstream, the other downstream – signifying the particular tensions of this age. The early symbol of Christianity, the religion which has changed the world more than any other, was also a fish.

Pisces has been marked by the meteoric influence of conquerors

from Alexander the Great to Adolf Hitler, each leaving a great swath of destruction and change in their wake.

How can ordinary people plan their lives in the face of the ravages of the next despot, or the assumptions made by the latest fashionable philosophy? Even democracy, with its supposed checks and balances, only allows the people to make their voice known once every few years. They have few other ways to give their consent to what is done in their name. The scales are still weighted on the side of the rulers, not the ruled.

Violent revolution is not an answer, since it destroys good and bad equally and, after its flame has passed by, its most extreme and brutal exponents are often in control – Robespierre after the French Revolution and Stalin after the Russian, for example.

Ours is a reactive society. It reacts to events *after* they have happened, because mechanisms do not exist for predicting them before they happen. An ancient, mocked belief in the existence of prediction lingers on, but modern methods of forecast, little more

Alexander the Great, whose conquests laid the foundations of the Piscean Age now passing

than projections, are today becoming more and more discredited. The reason is that, in the turbulence created by the dying of the three ages, our leaders can no more tell us what is going to happen next than the man in the moon!

It is no accident that in the past few years political systems, thought of almost as unchanging, have become as chaff in the wind.

Old certainties are unravelling before our eyes. What is happening now is not 'doom and gloom' prophecy, it is our present reality.

The execution of Louis XVI in 1793

Eastern Europe, shorn of Communism, is struggling to stay afloat in icy waters. The Soviet Union is no more — instead, republics with unfamiliar names jostle for recognition. The African continent is in political and ecological turmoil, while in South Africa the long supremacy of the whites seems to be coming to an uncertain end.

Where political systems remain intact, as in the West, the politicians that operate them appear helpless before events. Disillusionment with systems and performance has set in. Political uncertainties, unemployment and poverty are triggering off ethnic conflicts and social unrest and the continent of Europe is in danger of becoming destabilised. The civil war being waged in the Balkans threatens to draw in Muslim sympathisers to the east and EC countries to the west.

All over the world the old signposts are gone. We are witnessing not only the end of an era, but the birth of a new one. For that age to be born, old systems and beliefs must be swept away.

Great change in the next few years is inevitable, but change is often disturbing. Decisions which ought to be taken, plans which ought to be made, are 'frozen' by uncertainty over what is going to happen next.

Now Nostradamus will tell us all we need to know.

From 1995 onwards, the world's attention will focus on two countries — Britain and China — both headed for 'revolution', it is to be hoped, mainly peaceful.

China, the 'sleeping giant', will awaken to new democratic horizons and new alliances.

In Britain no echelon of government, from Parliament to local councils, from the House of Lords to the judiciary, will remain untouched. Systems and laws, in place for centuries, will vanish. The breakup of the United Kingdom is predicted.

China, the 'sleeping giant', will soon awaken

This transformation will result from two years of exciting politics beginning in 1994 and ending in a general election predicted for October 1995-March 1996. Against the background of this spectacular display of political fireworks, a legendary name in world politics will once more move to centre stage — Margaret Thatcher.

The former Prime Minister could prove to be the catalyst of events propelling a Labour and Liberal Democrat coalition government into office. While Paddy Ashdown's political star will shine, a surprise is that John Smith may not lead Labour to election victory.

Just as Britain is set to face constitutional revolution, so she will also undergo technological change, while social experiments will benefit a society racked by crime, poverty and inequality. Britain's 'new look' will become the model for many other nations. At the end of this process, Britain will emerge as the innovative design genius of a European superstate.

The global picture which these predictions unveil is one of many new situations, accompanied by some familiar and deep-seated problems. In the Middle East there will be a tragic war between Israel and the Arab states.

The next ten years will be characterised by the forming of economic power blocs of nations in several different regions, a prelude to world government in the next century.

Meanwhile, international uncertainty is set to continue up to the year 2000 when an era of peace and prosperity will gradually arrive.

Of prime importance during the next few years is the severe decline in the fortunes of the United States, following environmental setbacks and economic slump. It is not possible to see a revival before 2006.

Against the background of America's troubles, a new European star will be inexorably rising, as nations, including Britain, are compelled by circumstances to clear the path to political and economic union. Divisions will eventually melt away and European talent and creativity will flourish, particularly in science.

King of sciences will be physics linked to fantastic new technologies, enabling us to understand the universe, explore the powers of the mind and colonise the solar system. The same explosion in technological advance will enable us to enter a fabulous world of leisure.

On the horizon for medicine are advances in laser surgery,

more effective understanding of the causes of mental illness, new regimes of sport for the middle-aged and techniques for making possible rejuvenation. Also predicted is a cure for the modern scourge of AIDS.

A huge acceleration of knowledge will be experienced in many areas. Industrial pollution may end and care for the world's natural resources will produce major policies after the year 2000.

In characterising the nature of the next millennium, almost upon us, I would describe it in one word – exploration.

Over the next thousand years we will explore our galaxy. To equip ourselves for this great task – involving the possibility of encountering other intelligent races in space – we must also soon begin a great exploration of body, mind and spirit. Predictions tell of mind-strengthening technologies and a strange merging of physical science and spiritual belief, as the true nature of our universe becomes ever more clear.

As spiritual joins with physical, two halves of a single unity, it follows that this decade will eventually be viewed as the dying whisper of an age of darkness and ignorance.

V. J. Hewitt
March 1993

A detailed explanation of the decoding system appears at the end of this book, but the basic principle recognises that each original prophecy written by Nostradamus should be treated as an extended anagram.

The prophecy is first reduced to its basic components – letters – and then reassembled using a defined set of rules.

The method generates detailed predictions in French prose, together with the dating system which springs from the letters of the new predictions.

A list of the original prophecies used in this process appears at the end of this book.

Each new decoded prediction consists of French text, English translation, a dating display and my interpretation, followed by the date when the French prediction was decoded and the number of the original prophecy from which it emerged.

THE CRUCIBLE OF POLITICS

In which a lady lights a fire ...

Margaret Thatcher Ignites the Commons

Cinq: encore une fois, Margaret Thatcher fuse là-dedans la
           z
x   **s**   **s**   **s**   **u**
Chambre des Communes. L' idéologie met le feu à la politique
    s   **s**   **s**
vide. Desserre support au Major d'été raté.

"1995 onwards: once more Margaret Thatcher bursts forth inside
the House of Commons. Ideology sets alight the vacuum of politics. It loosens support for Major from a failed summer."

---

z	x	s	s	s	u	s	s	s
o	h	m	o	m	q	o	m	a
24	22	18	18	18	20	18	18	18
14	8	12	14	12	16	14	12	1
6	4	9	9	9	2	9	9	9
5	8	3	5	3	7	5	3	1
	10	Sept			9	Feb		99
May	11		95		Mar	7	95	Mar 1

I have chosen to begin with this prediction because it illustrates
the startling reason for much of the turbulence forecast for
British politics from the year 1995.

Prime Minister of Great Britain for eleven years during which
Communism disappeared from Eastern Europe and the Cold War
came to an end, Margaret Thatcher advocated a distinct political

and economic philosophy which became known the world over as 'Thatcherism'. She was forced to resign in November 1990, when Michael Heseltine challenged her for the leadership. John Major went on to defeat Heseltine.

In April 1992, the Conservative Party under Major's premiership won a fourth general election victory with a majority of 21 seats. In the same year, his predecessor entered the House of Lords as Baroness Thatcher.

Nevertheless, according to this and other predictions, it is by no means the end of Margaret Thatcher's career in the Commons.

It is predicted that she will re-enter the House of Commons as an elected Member of Parliament during 7 March 1995-9 February 1996. In order to do this, she would have to renounce her peerage and win a byelection.

Once there, her forthright and consistent defence of Thatcherism and her resistance to European political union will 'set alight a vacuum of ideas' in the Conservative Party. (One cannot 'set alight a vacuum'; it is scientifically impossible. However, the juxtaposition of incongruous and apparently inappropriate images to convey succinctly a profound truth is a consistent feature, not only of Nostradamus' prophecy, but prophecy in general, as an examination of prophetic passages in the Bible will confirm.) She will be aided by the fact that during 11 May–10 September, John Major's policies will be regarded as having failed. The economy may be in serious difficulties.

Her attacks on government policy could be seen as inflammatory and divisive, but during 1995 she may begin to draw party support away from John Major. At this point, her intervention would be crucial, since a general election would have to be called by the summer of 1997.

Another timetable may also be dictating events, one set by a European political agenda for 1996 onwards, with which Thatcher could profoundly disagree. Her aim would be to persuade the government and the country to reject this prospect.

The final date is 1 March 1999, which could mark a second retirement for this charismatic politician.

Margaret Thatcher at a military establishment in Cambridge, early on in her premiership, in the days of Molesworth and Greenham Common

April 1992 II. 51

Governor Patten Recalled from Hong Kong

A volatile period is predicted for John Major, beginning 1995. One cause of this turbulence appears to be the furore surrounding Margaret Thatcher as she emerges once more at the heart of British politics.

Chris Patten landing in Hong Kong at the start of his governorship there

Cinq: Chris Patten, gouvernor d'Hong Kong remballe, rappelé d'urgence par Major. Retourne au Royaume-Uni où la Dame de Fer frappe la politique après an furieux.

"1995 onwards: Chris Patten, governor of Hong Kong, prepares to leave, urgently recalled by Major. He returns to the United Kingdom where the Iron Lady strikes at politics after a furious year."

d	r	s	b	b	s	f	s	r	t	f	t	s	l	e
i	v	o	l	e	c	o	u	y	o	m	o	e	n	u
4	17	18	2	2	18	6	18	17	19	6	19	18	11	5
1:9	21	14	11	5	3	14	20	23	14	12	14	5	13	20
4	8	9	2	2	9	6	9	8	19	6	10	9	2	5
10	3	5	11	5	3	5	2	5	5	3	5	5	4	20
4	Aug					28	Aug			6	Oct		Feb	5
Oct	3	95	Nov	20					195	Mar	5	95	Apr	0
														0
														2

A key figure in the 1992 general election was Chris Patten, Conservative Party Chairman and the man credited with having guided the party to victory. Having lost his own seat, he was appointed the last Governor of Hong Kong before the handover of the colony to China in 1997. This is proving to be a sensitive, difficult assignment, so that only in extreme circumstances would John Major recall Chris Patten before that task was completed. One such reason could be the imminence of another general election, perhaps forced upon Major. Chris Patten might be recalled on two counts. Firstly, he could head the Conservative election campaign – a task fraught with nailbiting difficulty. Secondly, he may wish to stand as a candidate himself.

John Major waving to well-wishers from the first floor of Conservative Party Central Office, Smith Square, London, after hearing of the Conservative election victory on 9 April 1992. With him are his wife Norma and Chris Patten

It appears that Patten will still be Governor of Hong Kong on 3 October 1995, maintaining links with the colony until 4 August 1996.

Meanwhile, between 6 October 1995–5 March 1996, the 'Iron Lady' could be hitting the headlines.

From 20 November 1995, Patten could be recalled as a matter of urgency. A period of political uncertainty could follow, lasting until 28 August 1996 when decisions taken could mean that the Conservative Party remains out of power until February–April 2005.

Dating suggests that the general election could take place during 20 November 1995–5 March 1996.

If, as predicted, the Conservative government is replaced by a Labour_Liberal Democrat coalition, the new government may wish to replace Patten as Governor.

Tied in with these events could be the beginning of another major cycle of revolution in China (see 'China in Revolution – Tibet Freed').

April 1992 III. 53

Major Loses to Labour and Liberal Democrats

John Major, le chef du gouvernement britannique, son pouvoir

sera supplanté par les partis Labour et Liberal Democrat — un

gué au dessein pour décade.

*"John Major, the leader of the British government, his power
will be supplanted by the parties Labour and Liberal Democrat —
a ford to a design for the decade."*

s j	e n	s i	n a	s l	n t	g b	u t	s b	e t	s i	y o	e d
18	5	18	13	18	13	7	20	18	5	18	23	5
10	13	1:9	1	11	19	2	19	2	19	1:9	14	4
9	5	9	4	9	4	7	20	9	5	9	5	5
10	13	19	1	2	10	2	10	2	19	19	5	4
	95	199	Apr	Sep	4	Jul	2		95	199	5	May
Oct	13		Jan	Feb	0	Feb	0	Feb	19		May	4
					0		1					
					2		0					

THE prediction begins from 19 February 1995 when the
Liberal Democrats, acting from an increasingly strong base,
will vehemently oppose government policy. John Major is
still Conservative leader on 13 October, but time could be running out as a general election draws near.

A Lib–Lab coalition is predicted to defeat him.

During April 1999–January 2000, the British people may vote in an election or referendum – which could take place throughout the European Community during 4–5 May 1999 – to lose sovereignty and enter a European federation, the United States of Europe. This spectacular, continentwide union could be born in the year 2000. The decision will shape Britain's destiny for the next ten years.

During September 2004–February 2005, another election may see the British political scene fragmented by many parties winning seats under a system of proportional representation. A confused situation could continue until February–July 2010, when Labour could govern with the aid of one or more smaller parties.

Paddy Ashdown campaigning in March 1992

August 1991 III.65

Lib–Lab Pact Wins General Election

Cinq: après une élection générale que sème fruits sur Paddy Ashdown et Brown, la tête du partie* de Labour, le ministère miné quitte. Un axe que fait circuit à une cime.

"Cinq: after a general election that scatters fruits over Paddy Ashdown and Brown, the leader of the Labour Party, the undermined government quits. An axis that encircles a peak."

| s | s | f | s | y | s | m | f | q |
u	a	d	l	l	u	t	u	e
18	18	6	18	23	18	12	6	16
20	1	4	11	11	20	19	20	5
9	9	6	9	5	9	3	6	7
2	1	4	2	2	2	10	2	5
	99	96		95		3	6	Jul
Feb	1	4	Feb	2	Feb	0	Feb	5
						0		
						0		
						2		

*Partie means 'part', while *parti* refers to a political party. The word *partie* when applied to Labour may signify a split, after which Gordon Brown will lead a section of the Labour Party into an alliance with the Liberal Democrats. I have decoded several other predictions indicating a number of such fundamental realignments in British politics until at least AD 2000.

Paddy Ashdown during a news conference at the National Liberal Club in London

THE prediction foresees two developments in British politics during the next few years – a realignment of the political centreleft and a successful election victory of the coalition emerging from that realignment.

At the time of writing (1992) John Smith is Labour leader, but by the middle of the decade Gordon Brown may have replaced him.

Beginning 2 February 1995, a fundamental political shift begins. A pact could emerge between Labour and the Liberal Democrats and they may offer one candidate only to fight each Conservative at the next election; this could be called or take place around 4 February 1996. Paddy Ashdown could emerge as the driving force behind this alliance.

Gordon Brown may be the next leader of the Labour Party

The Lib–Lab pact could win enough seats to force out a divided Conservative government.

From 1 February 1999, another election or referendum becomes imminent. This political event will be even more crucial for the destiny of Britain. During 6 July 2003–5 February 2004 constitutional and social developments could well have transformed Britain.

NB: John Smith died 12 May 1994.

April 1992 X.89

Coup Threatens Conservative Leader

y p f u d
Cinq: à la Grande-Bretagne le partie* des Conservateurs sera

                                      n
renversé. Se lèseront en juin. Toisent l'Europe en mauvaise foi.
u f n m u t
Alors, un coup politique prend son essor muter chef.

"1995 onwards: in Great Britain the Conservative Party will be defeated. They will wound themselves in June. They regard Europe with dishonest scorn. Then a policital coup springs into life to transfer the leader."

y	p	f	u	d	n	u	f	n	m	u	t
a	g	a	a	a	v	a	i	e	e	e	e
23	15	6	20	4	13	20	6	13	12	20	19
1	7	1	1	1	21	1	1:9	5	5	5	5
5	6	6	2	4	4	2	6	4	3	2	19
1	7	1	1	1	3	1	19	5	5	5	5
May 6	6	Oct				2	196	4		May	
	9				5	Jan		Oct		5	195

DURING 1995–1996, a series of crises arises in the Conservative Party, culminating in the overthrow of John Major. Dating indicates that this will take place after the Conservatives have lost in the next general election. The cause is Europe, the Nemesis of the Conservatives over the last two decades.

* Partie — see note for previous prediction.

The party will find itself split from 5 October 1995, perhaps during the annual party conference, until 4 May 1996. Differences probably arise from moves to topple John Major as leader and 6 May 1996 could mark a turning point.

'They will wound themselves in June', could refer to June 1996 when a self-destructive political act may take place. This month could see schism in the Conservative Party with Tory MPs on the left switching their allegiance to another party.

The cause will be resentment among Conservative rightwingers of inevitable closer political union between European partners. By 1995, a highly politicised European agenda may be causing vehement opposition.

A political coup could be engineered by 2 April–5 January 1997, with a new leader emerging to head a smaller, rightwing, anti-European Conservative Party. (In 1991 I published a prediction that this leader would be Margaret Thatcher.)

Nostradamus predicts that John Major will lose the next election in 1995/6. A right-wing coup will replace him with Margaret Thatcher

April 1992 IX.36

Deception in the British Economy

f   *x*   *d*
Cinq: l'économie de la Grande Bretagne, il la faut juste

    p   *h*   *d*   *p*   *s*   *r*
évaluation. Au lieu de cela, vous rusez à surestimer hausse en

      s   *r*   *s*
dépreciations. Sert à mesestimer déficit.

"*1995 onwards — the economy of Great Britain needs a fair assessment. Instead, you deceive by overestimating the rise in depreciations. It serves to underestimate the deficit.*"

f	x	d	p	h	d	p	s	r	s	r	s
n	a	t	i	i	v	i	u	n	i	a	m
6	22	4	15	8	4	15	18	17	18	17	18
13	1	19	1:9	1:9	21	1:9	20	13	1:9	1	12
6	4	4	6	8	4	6	9	8	9	8	9
4	1	10	19	19	3	19	2	4	19	1	3
2	Apr	4	196	198	4	196	9	8	199	98	
0	1	Oct		Mar			Feb	Apr		1	Mar
0											
0											

NOSTRADAMUS uses the 'you' form when issuing a stern or significant warning — here, apparently, to the government(s) responsible for the British economy during 1995–2000.

During 1995, the economy could be an emotive issue, but in 1996 government figures could be issued around 9 February which give too optimistic a picture of the economy's prospects, possibly linked with a general election at this time.

The London Stock Exchange

This factor could be ignored as political excitement focuses on a survey later in the year, 4 April–1 October, of every aspect of government in Britain.

Around 1 March 1998, problems that spring from this earlier deception may begin to surface, while the government is carrying out wideranging and contentious reforms of monarchy, constitution and government in Britain. The government may realise that it has severely underestimated the amount of expenditure needed to carry out these reforms. From 4 March, figures could be issued that 'gloss' over the deficit.

The situation cannot be disguised for long because, around 8 April 1999, more than one devaluation of the currency may occur. This development may be connected with European monetary union, targeted for the end of the decade.

January 1992 II.51

BRITAIN'S REVOLUTION

... and a new Britain rises from the flames ...

Charles Fights to Keep Royal Powers

---

p   b   s   f   d   a
Cinq: Charles Troisième se heurte à l'opposition publique à la
u   s   t   b   r   a
monarchie. Rex se braque contre le gouvernement que se met sus
u   r   t   q u
à refondre le bagage de Parlement. Tue le but dur.

"1995 onwards: Charles III encounters public opposition to the
monarchy. The King stubbornly resists the government which
begins in a rush to overhaul the baggage of Parliament. He kills
off the tough purpose."

---

p	b	s	f	d	a	u	s	t	b	r	a	u	r	t	l	q	u
n	h	r	h	n	i	o	e	c	n	e	m	n	e	e	n	e	e
15	2	18	6	4	1	20	18	19	2	17	1	20	17	19	11	16	20
13	8	17	8	13	1:9	14	5	3	13	5	12	13	5	5	13	5	5
6	2	9	6	4	1	2	9	19	2	19	1	2	8	19	2	7	2
4	8	8	8	4	19	5	5	3	4	5	3	4	5	5	4	5	5
6	Feb		June 7					19 Feb			1	Oct			2	Jul	2
Apr	8	98	8 Apr			195	95	Mar	4	195		Jul		5	195	5 May	
															0		
															0		
															4		

47

EVIDENTLY the year 1995 begins a very difficult period for the British monarchy. The King's problems may begin with the election of a radical government in 1995–6. The new administration will aim to reform many aspects of government, including the constitutional monarchy, a movement which may have begun to have an impact well before, since Charles seems to resist the idea throughout 1995.

Whatever the political complexion of the government, between 4 March 1995–19 February 1996, he will find himself at odds with what is proposed – a stance that may make his position uncertain as he encounters a hardening public attitude to the trappings and privileges of monarchy (7 June 1995–8 April 1996). These difficulties will be accompanied by a rising tide of belief that unreformed government in all its aspects is preventing the British from reaching their full potential.

In response, 5 July–1 October 1995 may see the passing of hurried measures getting rid of some constitutional 'baggage', but these could be viewed as superficial, compared with what is needed.

Although he may have to relinquish certain privileges, the King's resistance may postpone fundamental reform of the monarchy for some years, while public attention may begin to shift to Prince William as England's next King. By 8 April 1998–6 February 1999, the spotlight is divided equally between Charles and William.

The final period is 5 May–2 July 2004 when Parliament may finally push through these belated reforms. This development is predicted to occur during the reign of William the Fifth and may spell the end of the constitutional powers of the monarchy.

Prince Charles will soon face a fresh struggle to retain royal power and privilege

Diana Blunts Public Hostility

T HROUGHOUT 1995, public opinion will be hostile to the monarchy, with Queen Diana finding that this mood has particular meaning for her during 7 October 1995–1 April 1996.

---

    g   *ʃ z*   *ʃ g d*   *t*

Cinq: la reine Diana se voue à émousser l'herse d'opinion

     d a t   *d et*   *s s s*

publique hostile à la monarchie, afin qu'elle sauve le trone pour

uu *t*   *c c*   *s*

William. Rex se jette dans les erreurs.

"1995 onwards: Queen Diana dedicates herself to blunting the harrow of public opinion hostile to the monarchy, that she may save the throne for William. The King throws himself into errors."

---

g	f	z	f	g	d	t	d	a	t	d	e	t	s	s	s	t	c	c	s
i	n	i	u	o	l	o	q	i	l	h	n	q	v	n	o	i	n	l	u
7	6	24	6	7	4	19	4	1	19	4	5	19	18	18	18	19	3	3	18
1:9	13	1:9	20	14	11	14	16	1:9	11	8	13	16	21	13	14	1:9	13	11	20
7	6	6	6	7	4	19	4	1	10	4	5	19	9	9	9	10	3	3	9
19	4	19	2	5	2	5	7	10	11	8	4	7	3	4	5	10	4	11	2

197	6	196		13Apr		Apr 1		14	May		9 Sep			2000			6 Sep	
Apr			Feb 7		195	7 Oct		Nov 12		197	Mar 4	95		2000			15 Feb	

Princess Diana may dedicate herself to safeguarding Prince William's path to the throne

During the years 1995–2000 her concern may be for Prince William's future, as the King 'throws himself into errors'. Charles may not take fully into account the depth of opposition and makes a series of public relations errors. Alternatively, in order to combat a number of false assumptions about the monarchy, he will have to throw himself into the task of correcting them. The period 15 February–6 September 2000 will be of crucial importance to Prince William, as it may indicate the period when he will become King. Predictions indicate that the reign of Charles III could be so unpopular as to compel a transfer of rule from Charles to William in order to prevent the monarchy from being abolished.

Between 13 April 1996–7 February 1997 Queen Diana could dedicate herself to softening public resentment, from concern that the fourteen-year-old Prince William's path to the throne could be in jeopardy.

Around 6 April 1997 media attention could focus on Diana and William. A monarchist movement may spring up aiming to make William King at an early age, say, in the year 2000 when he is eighteen, or in 2003 when he is twenty-one.

While Queen Diana might not give active support to such a movement, she could be viewed as its figurehead, particularly during 12 November 1997–14 May 1998, a period connected with later predictions that Scotland will become a fully independent state. Such a development would pose a constitutional crisis for King Charles, ruler of both England and Scotland, then effectively two separated countries.

As early as 4 March–9 September 1995 the monarchy could find itself in crisis over the issue of the succession and the survival of the monarchy.

September 1992 II.51

The End of the British Monarchy?

t   d   f   b   p
Cinq: le parlement érige la constitution au dessus de la voix de
b   b   b f g   r   r
la monarchie britannique. Plus tard, les us et coutumes royals,
r   b   r   a   r   q   u
sans mérite, braquent le peuple qui les gèle.

"1995: Parliament raises the constitution above the voice of the British monarchy. Later on, royal habits and customs, without merit, antagonise the people who freeze them."

t	d	f	b	p	b	b	b	f	g	r	r	r	b	r	a	r	q	u
n	i	n	s	i	n	n	s	d	l	c	y	n	i	n	l	i	s	l
19	4	6	2	15	2	2	2	6	23	17	17	17	2	17	1	17	16	20
13	1:9	13	18	1:9	13	13	18	4	11	3	23	13	19	13	11	1:9	18	11
10	4	6	2	6	2	2	2	10	5	8	17	8	2	8	1	8	7	2
13	10	4	9	19	4	4	9		11	3	5	4	10	4	11	19	18	11
Oct	12			196		4	Feb	2	May	25		98	2	Aug	1	198	Jul	2
		27	Sep	Apr	13			0		11	Mar		0	Apr	Nov		18	0
								0					1					1
								0					0					1

THIS prediction spells out the end of the British monarchy in its present form between 1996–2011. During 12 October 1996–27 September 1997 Parliament will introduce a new constitution making the monarch answerable to the same laws and taxes as the ordinary citizen – but also possessing the same rights, such as the vote. I have assumed that the 'parliament' referred to by the prediction is the Westminster parliament, although it is possible that the European parliament may have grown so powerful by this time that it could impose a new constitution upon Britain.

In subsequent years we could see a hardening resentment of the British people, still affected by memories of a recession which began with the decade, against an outmoded monarchy and its remaining privileges. Nevertheless, changes may not be considered before 1998, reasons being the huge programme of reform proposed for other areas of government and the resistance of the monarchy.

It is not until 25 May 1998–11 March 1999 that royal 'habits and customs', the trappings of privilege, may once more come under scrutiny, with calls to have them abolished. 1 November 1998 may mark a turning-point in this process, with public opinion winning.

During 13 April 2000–4 February 2001 the British monarchy may be in the headlines. I have decoded a number of predictions in the last two years which indicate that Prince William could become King William V on, or around, his birthday on 21 June 2000.

This development could be seen as a last-ditch attempt to retain royal power and privilege with the advent of a popular, young King. However, in years to come, such privilege may be regarded as anachronistic. During April–August 2010 public opinion may think it right to remove inherited privilege from any individual – a development that could spell out the end of the aristocratic class, with the monarchy eventually resembling modern European monarchies. An individual's personal merit may become the only path to privilege.

Around 18 July 2011, all such inherited privileges, including those of the King, could be suspended or abolished.

July 1993 I.28

Queen Elizabeth II on her way to the State opening of Parliament

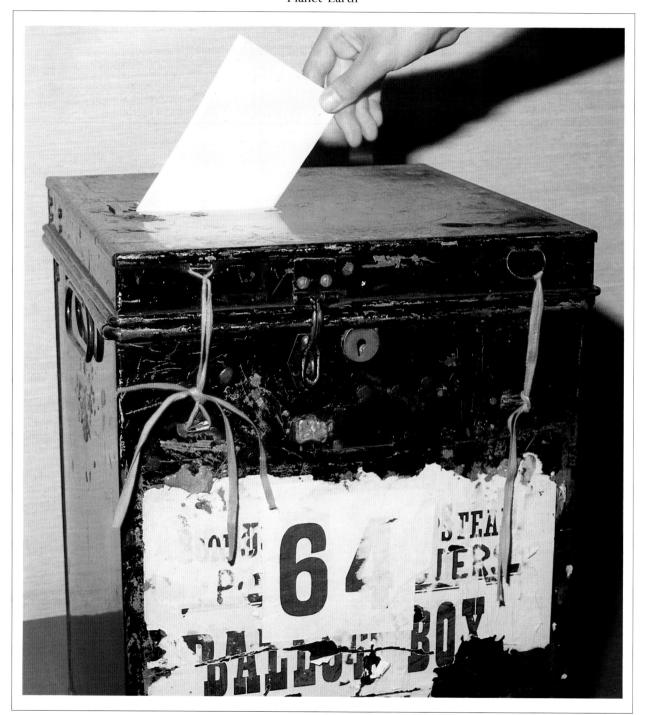

Public Rejoices over New Voting System

Dramatic changes are forecast for the British electoral system

---

b   u   b   k   ƒ
Cinq: le système change à l'une de représentation

r   r   r ƒ   r   r
proportionnelle. Le fait paraphé produit des gens gambadés,

ƒ   m   a   u   u   g
jusqu'à Rex, avides de lui participer. Fort rural.

"1995 onwards: the system changes to one of proportional representation. The signed act produces a people jumping for joy, all
the way up to the King, eager to take part. A rural fortress."

THE prediction emphasises the 'joy' and sudden release as a
new electoral system extends the vote to all British citizens, including peers of the realm and the King.
Britain currently uses the 'first past the post' system, while other

b	u	b	k	f	r	r	r	f	r	r	f	m	a	u	u	g
i	y	c	e	i	o	t	e	o	s	d	s	v	i	i	t	l
2	20	2	—	6	17	17	17	6	17	17	6	12	1	20	20	7
19	23	3	5	19	14	19	5	14	18	4	18	21	19	19	19	11
2	20	2	—	6	17	8	8	6	8	8	6	12	1	20	20	7
19	5	3	5	19	5	19	5	5	9	4	9	3	19	10	10	11
Feb	20	Feb	196	17	8	Aug 6	98	8	96	12	Jan			2	2	Jul
	195	3 May			May19	5 May			Apr		Mar19			0	0	11
														1	1	
														0	0	

countries in the EC employ different forms of proportional representation. Around 20 February 1995, our political system will be debated increasingly.

During February–3 May 1996, the British government will introduce a system following those on the Continent.

By 17 May 1998, further changes to the electoral system could be envisaged, but it may not be until 6 August 1998–5 May 1999 that the form of voting in Britain is permanently fixed. This may be connected with an agreement in the EC (now probably much larger than at the beginning of the decade) to have a uniform method of voting for all member countries.

A general election or referendum using this fixed system could take place in all member states during 1999. The 'signed act' may refer to monetary and political union, following the consent of the peoples of Europe, transforming the Community into a United States of Europe in 2000.

The prediction then highlights the next decade when all voters, despite past disillusionment or apathy, may be eager to take part in the electoral process. Voting may take place through home computer links and electors could be consulted regularly on major questions.

The 'rural fortress' emerging around 11 July 2010 is the first of two references in this section to a transfer of power to people living outside British cities. It may indicate an accelerated move to the countryside, as people adapt to working at home, or within their immediate area. Land reform, highlighted for this period, could also have a connection.

September 1992 III.53

England – A Written Constitution

h   h   p   u
Cinq: une nouvelle constitution écrite pour l'Angleterre fait
p   h   P   h   p o   u   b
citoyens avec droits des gens. Pousse Rex. Il devient soumis à loi
h   p   u   u   s   r   s
de la terre, forcé de payer des taxes.

"1995 onwards: a new, written constitution for England creates citizens with rights from the people. It puts pressure on the King. He becomes subject to the law of the land, obliged to pay taxes."

BRITAIN has never had a written constitution, but within a few years this situation will change for England, while Scotland will be making her own arrangements. Spectacular constitutional developments are also predicted for Wales.

During 4 March–20 February 1996, much pressure from government and people will be placed upon the King to 'normalise' his tax situation. Queen Elizabeth II gave a promise through Parliament at the end of 1992 to pay income tax, but this offer remains voluntary and the monarchy is still exempt from other forms of duty, notably inheritance taxes. By 20 February 1996, King Charles will be obliged to pay all the taxes imposed upon the ordinary citizen, but he will still not possess the same status, being exempt from many acts passing through Parliament.

During 8 August 1996–11 April 1997, a written constitution could be created for England, taking the social and technological demands of the age into account. Because resistance will come from King Charles over provisions within the constitution which relate to the monarchy, the public may begin to focus on his son Prince William as their next King. William will be eighteen in the year 2000.

Around 8 May 1996, the King will be under heavy pressure to comply. Following 12 May 1996–24 April 1997, he will become subject to the law of the land, just like any other citizen. From 17 April 1999, he may be obliged to pay new taxes.

Reforms will continue for several years. Between 24 July 2005–23 June 2006, the new constitution will finally have 'created citizens with rights' from a people whose legal status has hardly changed as subjects of the monarchy since medieval times.

The Lincoln Memorial in Washington. Britain will follow America in drawing up a written constitution

September 1992 VII. 14

h	h	p	u	p	h	p	h	p	o	u	b	h	p	u	u	s	r	s
l	n	i	e	y	a	g	e	i	d	i	i	d	t	c	d	y	d	t
8	8	15	20	15	8	15	8	15	14	20	2	8	15	20	20	18	17	18
11	13	19	5	23	1	7	5	19	4	19	19	4	19	3	4	23	4	19
8	8	6	2	6	8	15	8	6	5	2	2	8	6	20	2	9	17	9
11	4	19	5	23	1	7	5	19	4	10	10	4	19	3	4	5	4	19
Aug	8	196	2	Jun	23		8	196	May	12			196	20	Feb		17	199
11	Apr		0				May		Apr	24				Mar	4	95		Apr
			0	24			Jul											
			5															

House of Lords Abolished

u   g   p   a   p   p   h   k   f
Cinq: la réforme de Parlement embrasse les procedures, aussi bien

p r   r   f   r   p   r   f   t
que l'abolition de la Chambre des Lords. Tant de pouvoir

u   u   n   g   a
transféré aux regions. Rex jugeable.

"1995 onwards: the reform of Parliament includes the procedures, as well as the abolition of the House of Lords. So much
power transferred to the regions. The King subject to judgement
in court."

BETWEEN 16 June 1996–February 1997, a great raft of
constitutional reforms will be introduced by the government of the day. Many procedures will be modernised.
During 30 June–14 December, the government will introduce
measures to abolish the House of Lords, perhaps to be replaced

| u | g | p | a | p | p | h | k | f | p | r | r | f | r | p | r | f | t | u | u | n | g | a |
c	o	e	e	b	s	o	s	i	e	l	o	l	m	s	o	d	v	x	i	e	b
20	7	15	1	15	15	8	—	6	15	17	17	6	17	15	17	6	19	20	20	13	7	1
3	14	5	5	2	18	14	18	19	5	11	14	11	12	18	14	4	21	18	22	19	5	2
20	7	6	1	15	6	8		6	6	8	8	6	8	6	8	10	10	20	20	4	7	1
3	5	5	5	2	9	14	9	19	5	2	5	2	12	9	5		3	9	4	19		7
2	Jul	Jun	16	96	Aug		196	Jun	30						96	Aug	2	Oct	2	2	Apr	8
0	May	10		Feb	14 Sep								14 Dec			May	0	Mar	0	0		197
0																	0		0	0		
3																	0		9	4		

**The House
of Lords**

by an elected second Chamber, though this is not clear. August—14 September could be an important period.

By 8 April 1997, further measures will establish self-governing assemblies in regions of England and make the monarchy subject to the laws of the land with equal responsibilities and rights.

After the year 2000, reforms will focus on the possible abolition of hereditary titles, except for the monarchy. During 2003 —2009 there may be another great period of reform transforming power to the people from entrenched vested interests.

September 1992 III.53

Britain's Secrecy Laws Repealed

j f   f   z f   x
Cinq: On révèle beaucoup de matières après l'abrogation des
h h   d   s   s   s   e
lois britanniques du secret, malgré de la corruption a été
u   s   s   e   s
detruit par lacération. Lui messied.

"1995 onwards: many matters come to light after the repeal of British secrecy laws, although some corruption has been put through the shredder. An unbecoming sight."

BRITAIN has the most secretive government in the Western world. Over two hundred laws relate to the keeping of secrets in numerous areas judged by many to be outside the requirements of the national interest. Reform, including a Bill of Rights and a Freedom of Information Act, has long been advocated.

During January–August 1995, evidence of official corruption, previously suppressed, may come to light. Papers connected with this revelation may be 'put through the shredder' to prevent public disclosure. This destruction of documents may, or may not, become known during 1995, but between 12 October 1996–29 May 1997 many more secrets could emerge, accompanied by rising public anger over being kept in the dark.

j	f	f	z	f	x	h	h	d	s	s	s	e	u	s	s	e	s
q	n	o	i	p	b	o	b	c	r	a	o	t	i	r	n	i	i
10	6	6	24	6	22	8	8	4	18	17	18	5	20	18	18	5	18
16	13	14	1:9	15	2	14	2	3	17	1	14	19	1:9	17	13	1:9	1:9
10	6	6	6	6	4	8	8	4	9	8	9	5	2	9	9	5	9
16	13	5	19	6	2	14	2	3	8	1	5	10	19	8	4	19	19
Oct	12	196			26 Apr				Aug		5 Feb			Sep	195	199	
	29 May		Jun	21			98		Jan 95		Oct 19		98 Apr				

A number of secrecy laws could have been repealed by 21 June 1998–26 April 1999. The timescale suggests that considerable resistance from the Establishment will delay this process, but it is difficult to overestimate the impact that information previously concealed will have, both on areas of government and on how people view their leaders.

Nevertheless, more documents could be destroyed during 19 October 1998–5 February 1999. Despite such acts, the year 1999 may see revealed a catalogue of ill-considered, incompetent and corrupt deeds committed over many decades.

The Public Records Office in London, where official government papers are released to the public

September 1992 II.51

Shock Secrets Force Judicial Reform

Cinq: Le ressentiment des gens fuse à la lumière des coups de **z**

secrets. On fait la réforme hative de la judiciaire au but de **g** **x** **h** **p**

réserver la réputation de la justice. **s** **s** **o** **s**

"1995 onwards: The resentment of the people bursts forth in the light of shocks from secrets. The hurried reform of the judiciary takes place with the aim of saving the reputation of justice."

z	g	x	h	p	s	s	o	s
e	t	i	i	i	v	n	e	j
24	7	22	8	15	18	18	14	18
5	19	1:9	1:9	19	21	13	5	10
6	7	4	8	6	9	9	5	9
5	19	10	19	19	3	4	5	19
6	197	4	198	196	9		95	199
May		Oct			Mar	Apr	5	

5 April 1995 may see the reputation of the judiciary in danger of being damaged. Around 9 March 1996 far-reaching reforms could be proposed. These may be dropped, due to the resistance of judges.

However, following the repeal of secrecy laws (see previous prediction) the anger of the people may know no bounds as many disreputable secrets within the legal system emerge into the public domain (6 May 1997).

This situation will raise acute problems of public confidence. In response, a series of fundamental reforms could be rushed through by 4 October 1998.

'Equal justice for all' will be a theme running throughout 1999.   January 1993 II.51

Land Reform Grants Public Access

```
d   d       h       h      m    m                 h
```
Cinq: lois nouvelles concernant de propriété foncière autorisent
```
d     o     d          h       u     o             u o
```
un droit publique de passage aux terres rurales, même palais de
```
c    a    a    m  a    o
```
Rex. L'âge dur de campagne.

"1995 onwards: new laws relating to land ownership authorise a public right of access to country estates, even the King's palaces. A lasting age of the countryside."

| d | d | h | h | m | m | h | d | o | d | h | u | o | u | o | c | a | a | m | a | o |
q	i	s	n	p	f	n	n	i	q	e	e	r	i	e	r	l	e	r	e	p
4	4	8	8	12	12	8	4	14	4	8	20	14	20	14	3	1	1	12	1	14
16	1:9	18	13	15	6	13	13	1:9	16	5	5	17	1:9	5	17	11	5	17	5	15
4	4	8	8	3	12	8	4	5	4	8	20	5	20			10	3	1		5
16	10	9	4	6	6	4	4	19	7	5	5	17	10	5	17	11	5	8	5	6
Apr	4	98		Aug 27				195	4 Aug	2		May 2			2					9
16 Oct				20 Apr				Jul 5		0	17	0	May28		0			Aug 5		6
										0		1			0					
										5		0			5					

DURING 27 August 1995–20 April 1996, a nationwide movement may spring up, demanding public access to private land, much of which may be lying fallow under the European Community 'set aside' policy. This rewards farmers for reducing production of certain crops.

The Pennine Way, County Durham

The vast portion of land in Britain is owned by about 10 per cent of the population and it could be that in the period of sweeping reforms predicted in this section public access to privately owned land may become an emotive issue.

Around 5 August 1996, a new Act of Parliament may compel landowners to introduce measures to protect the countryside. During 4 April–16 October 1998, there could be as many as five new laws, giving access to private land.

Between 5 July–4 August 2005, acts of land reform could involve the state taking over huge estates, with special emphasis on royal lands occurring around 28 May. 'The age of the king' could mean that, with this new law, royal lands and houses may pass from any control by the monarchy.

Certainly, by 17 May 2010, many royal palaces could even have become public museums, housing art collected by British Kings and Queens over centuries. By this time, if it still exists, the monarchy could have become a much smaller, less grand and powerful influence.

September 1992 IV.44

Scotland Wins Independence

   x   *s*   *t*   *h*   *d*
Cinq: l'arreté haut du roi. L'indépendance pour l'Écosse, un des

          b   *d*   *x*   *h*   *u*
astres européens. Le dommage — chemin économique à l'air rude

     d   *a*   *o*
au moignon devant tour à la campagne.

"1995 onwards: a high decree from the King. Independence for Scotland, one of the European stars. Damage — an economic path seems rugged to the amputated stump before the walk in the open countryside."

x	s	t	h	d	b	d	x	h	u	d	a	o
q	e	i	n	n	e	e	n	q	i	n	n	n
22	18	19	8	4	2	4	22	8	20	4	1	14
16	5	1:9	13	13	5	5	13	16	1:9	13	13	13
4	9	19	8	4	2	4	4	8	20	4	1	5
7	5	10	4	4	5	5	4	7	19	4	4	4
Apr			198		6		Aug		2	4	Jan	
7	95	Oct	4	Sep		16			0	98		
									1			
									0			

NOSTRADAMUS' habit of using dramatic and incongruous imagery to describe a complex situation in a few words is seen here in full flow, with the picture of 'the amputated stump' of Scotland, cut off from the main body of Britain, trying to climb the rugged path of economic independence before reaching softer open ground.

A bridge in Scotland bearing graffiti of the Scottish National Party

The Act of Union of 1707 bound together the two ancient kingdoms of England and Scotland, together with the princedom of Wales, within the United Kingdom of Great Britain. It will be the task of Charles III to sign the royal decree setting Scotland free to go her own way.

The date that sets off this hugely complex process is 7 April 1995, although the many legal and constitutional problems will take several years to solve – until 4 October 1998.

Scotland will be represented by a new star on the European Community flag. At present, the decision is to have only twelve stars adorning the flag, despite the numbers of other countries joining. This decision may be changed, due to pressure from new members.

Despite the current belief in Scotland that she would very quickly become viable after independence, her economy could be severely hindered by the breakup. Nevertheless, the hardy Scottish people will scent the heady air of independence and head for the political uplands. It is likely that her economy will not achieve its full potential until 16 September 2010–6 August 2011, although by this time she could be a leading member of the European Community.

February 1992 IV.44

Self-Government for English Regions

> x h h
> Cinq: l'Angleterre pousse séparatisme moderé pour les regions
> $b\,d$ x h u u d
> à la constitution nouvelle que s'arroge un droit de la campagne
> c m n
> au delà du code, hors macadam.

> "1995 onwards — England pursues moderate separatism for her regions under a new constitution that assumes a right of the countryside beyond the law and outside tarmac."

x	h	h	b	d	x	h	u	u	d	c	m	n
q	s	i	n	n	q	s	n	l	g	l	e	r
22	8	8	2	4	22	8	20	20	4	3	12	13
16	18	1:9	13	13	16	18	13	11	7	11	5	17
4	8	8	2	4	4	8	20	20	4	3	3	4
7	9	19	4	4	7	9	4	2	7	2	5	8
4	98	198	Jun		4	98	2	2				104
Jul			4		Nov		0	0				
							0	0	Sept		13	
							4	2				

ENGLAND, by 1998 politically separated from Scotland, will acquire a written constitution.

Under this new statutory declaration of rights, English regions will become moderately self-governing, with their own regional assemblies. This development appears to occur during 1998, possibly after 4 July.

The details of the constitution will have been already hammered out in political debate between 4 June–4 November 1998.

The prediction then appears to 'jump' to 2002–2004, by which time important principles enshrined in the constitution will have ensured that the welfare of the environment has become paramount in the political process, overriding any law and consequently any project involving the construction of roads and buildings.

A poppy field in Suffolk

Of particular significance is the date 13 September 2004.

February 1992 IV.44

A New Constitution for Wales

b   *x*   *m*   *t*
Cinq: le Pays de Galles, une territoire que se fie à sa

    y   *t*   *t*   *m*   *p*
constitution ferme. Un plan quinquennal que dure assez long

    s   *m*   *i*   *i*   *u*
d'humer liberté. Cardiff au centre d'une renaissance.

*"1995 onwards: in Wales a governed territory that trusts in its
firm constitution and a five-year plan that lasts long enough to
scent liberty. Cardiff at the centre of a renaissance."*

TOGETHER with England and Scotland, Wales will undergo a constitutional revolution during the next decade, although the last vestiges of English control do not seem likely to fall away until 2 April 2004 when Wales could become a fully-fledged nation state.

b	x	m	t	y	t	t	m	p	s	m	i	i	u
n	l	r	a	n	l	l	z	g	l	n	d	n	a
2	22	12	19	23	19	19	12	15	18	12	1:9	1:9	20
13	11	17	1	13	11	11	2	7	11	13	4	13	1
2	4	12	19	5	19	19	3	6	9	3	19	19	20
4	2	8	1	4	2	2	2	7	2	4	4	4	1
2004	Dec	195		2000	Mar		96	Mar		2000			2
Apr 2	Aug 5			Feb 2		9	Feb	Apr 8					0
													0
													1

Wales has been a fiefdom of the English Crown for centuries and the eldest son of the reigning monarch of England and Scotland traditionally becomes Prince of Wales. However, with Scotland predicted to achieve full independence in this decade and much political power being devolved to English regional assemblies, the debate on Welsh independence will rank high on the agenda.

A new constitution for Wales will begin to be devised between 5 August–December 1995. It could be in place during March 1996–9 February 1997, lasting several years and becoming the foundation of her eventual independence.

Beginning in the year 2000, a new five-year economic and political plan for Wales will generate confidence in her ability to take her place among the members of the EC.

During 8 April 2000–March 2001, Cardiff, the capital of Wales, could be at the heart of a cultural renaissance. The city could also become the site of a Welsh Parliament by 2001.

Wales could achieve statehood by 2 April 2004, in the reign of William V, while acknowledging him as her King (see next prediction).

A room in Cardiff Castle. The city will symbolise political and cultural change for Wales

February 1992 X.89

King William V of England

v   pp   b   uu c   h   s   n   o
Après l'an deux mille William — fils de Charles Rex et la reine
s   t p   o   u   n   t
Diana — sera le souverain fort d'Angleterre; or Écosse, coupée,
*   u   v   t   s*
choisit une autre philosophie politique.

"After the year 2000, William — son of King Charles and Queen Diana — will be the steadfast sovereign of England; but Scotland, severed, chooses another political philosophy."

SCOTLAND, an independent nation state at the end of the decade, will not have William as her king. Whether she selects a ruler of her own, or becomes a republic, is not revealed, but the latter is more likely.

However, William will prove to be a loyal and steadfast King of England.

Around 18 April 1995, attention may, at first, focus on Queen Diana and other women in the royal family, but could then switch from 11 April to the inevitable separation of England and Scotland and the changes this severance will wreak upon the British constitution.

Between May 1996–12 January 1997, public debate will concentrate on the practical difficulties. Interest could fasten on Prince William as the next King of England, with some advocating his taking the throne early to prevent Scotland breaking away altogether.

During 18 April–11 November 1998, this proposal could be seized upon as a last-ditch attempt to stop the inevitable, but during 22 February–20 November 1998, the Scottish people could firmly reject the prospect, either through their Parliament,

Prince William is set to become the focus of a new royalist movement

or by referendum, of sharing a King with England. Legal separation of the two countries could become a reality this year.

Around 3 February 2000, the movement to place William on the English throne could become overwhelming, signifying that resistance to the monarchy of Charles III is producing a strong republican mood. The prediction indicates that by 2004, the young King could be providing a steady anchor for the English people.

v	p	p	b	c	h	s	n	o	s	t	p	o	u	n	t	u	v	t	s
a	l	a	i	i	i	l	l	i	d	a	l	a	d	l	e	i	a	l	i
21	15	15	2	3	8	18	13	14	18	19	15	14	20	13	19	20	21	19	18
1	11	1	1:9	1:9	1:9	11	11	1:9	4	1	11	1	4	11	5	1:9	1	11	1:9
21	15	15	2	3	8	18	4	5	18	19	6	5	20	4	19	2	21	1	9
1	11	1	10	10	19	11	11	19	4	1	11	1	4	11	5	19	1	11	19
				Feb 3		8	18		Apr 5	18			196	May 2		Apr 19		Feb 22	9
				2000		19	Nov11		19	Apr			Jan	12	0	11	5	20 Nov	19
															0				
															4				

See Note

Note: Famous people either change the course of history through their deeds and words, or they come to represent significant symbols of such changes. Monarchs belong in both categories.

Confirmation of this significance often occurs in the dating system of predictions about them. The relevant numbers here are:

21	15	15
1	11	1

Going clockwise, 21:15 = 21:6, or 21 June – Prince William's birthday. The remaining numbers – 15, 1, 11, 1 – make 28. Reversed, this is the number 82, or 1982, the year of his birth. The fact that this numerical riddle occurs in the phrase 'After the year', followed by the date 3 February 2000, suggests that William could become King on 21 June 2000, when he is eighteen.

S O C I E T Y

In a world where the individual shapes society ...

A New Deal for Women

En la société, les femmes ordinaires ne taisant plus au sujet de (x g · q · g f)

leur asservissement caduc. Cherchent calculer le nouvel droit (b · d · b · i a d a)

d'aînesse politique. (a · i)

"In society, ordinary women are no longer silent about their null and void enslavement. They seek to calculate the new political birthright."

x	g	q	g	f	b	d	b	i	a	d	a	a	i
e	e	s	s	j	s	u	r	r	e	v	o	s	u
22	7	16	7	6	2	4	2	1:9	1	4	1	1	1:9
5	5	18	18	10	18	20	17	17	5	21	14	18	20
4	7	7	7	6	2	4	2	19	1	4	1		20
5	5	9	9	1	9	2	8	8	5	3	5	9	2
Apr	7	97	97	6		6	Feb		19=2000			Sep	2
5	May			Jan	Sep	10		198					0
													0
													2

A worldwide protest movement is triggered off at the ballot box, not by highly articulate, educated or wealthy women, but by those millions of ordinary women who look after homes, rear children, care for sick and elderly relatives, do charitable work – essential tasks never costed by governments into national expenditure.

Precise legal terms indicate that this situation, viewed as out-of-date in a modern society, will be gradually replaced by a new political framework which each woman will enter at birth.

Women will soon be in charge of many areas of society

From 6 January 1997, the first signs occur that women do not intend to remain silent. By 7 April–5 May, the role of women in society is being hotly debated, sparked off by social and political changes affecting Britain and many other countries.

January 1991 I.42

From 10 September 1998–6 February 1999, a study assesses the 'hidden value' to society of caring work carried out by women. This review could anticipate the year 2000 when women will achieve 'a new right' – perhaps discarding outdated ideas about the ideal structure of society.

By September 2002, women equipped with a political birthright will live in a society that is highly technological, but flexible and more responsive to individual needs. Its priorities will often surprise those born in an earlier age.

Technology Transforms Education

r o m r d f o a
Cinq: à l'Angleterre l'éducation des enfants use technologie
f o r c a   c o q a
nouvelle de stimuler le cerveau bafré — apprend le savoir avec
*   r*
parfaite aisance.

"1995 onwards: in England children's education uses new technology to stimulate the greedy brain — it learns knowledge with perfect ease."

OVER a period of twelve years education in England is transformed and a new generation grows up with dramatically increased powers of learning. Britain is predicted to become the innovative genius of Europe and this forecast may well explain that development.

From April 1996, education comes under the spotlight with many radical innovations designed to remedy faults in the system. New techniques could extend to the use of advanced computing networks, Virtual Reality and fibre optics, as well as equipment not yet developed. Between May 1996–24 March 1997, technology will be widely employed in child and adult education.

Applications grow by leaps and bounds. By 17 May 1998–14 March 1999, technology transmits knowledge in ways tailored perfectly to individual needs. Teachers will have to meet the challenge of an alarmingly brilliant generation, original, creative and unorthodox to the point of genius.

As they grow up, absorbed knowledge will re-emerge from these children in a variety of dazzling theories, inventions and designs of great social benefit.

r	o	m	r	d	f	o	a	f	o	r	c	a	c	o	q	a	r
n	l	t	u	e	n	e	t	v	e	u	e	v	e	l	v	v	t
17	14	12	17	4	6	14	1	6	14	17	3	1	3	14	16	1	17
13	11	19	20	5	13	5	19	21	5	20	5	21	5	11	21	21	19
8	14	12	8	9	6	5	1	6	19	8	3	1	3	5	16	1	8
13	11	10	20		4	5	19	3		20	5	21	5	11	3	3	19
Aug	26	8			96	May 1		196		8		4 Mar		May 17			198
		0			Apr		24 Mar			0	May 26				14 Mar		
		0								0							
	24 Oct	2								2							

Fears of possible 'burnout' may not come to anything, since the brain will always be learning at its own pace. The boredom with lessons plaguing generations of schoolchildren ever since Shakespeare wrote of the boy that creeps unwillingly to school will swiftly become a thing of the past.

Ten years later, English education may be the model for many other countries. Evidence during 4 March–26 May 2008 suggests that new technology will stimulate young brains to gain knowledge even faster. During 26 August–26 October this evidence becomes public.

A social problem could emerge, in that the new generation may become intellectual giants at an early age – how will they then regard their 'ordinary' parents?

**Computer in a
Japanese kindergarten**

September 1992 VIII.4

The Criminal Reformed

    x   s   n

Cinq: beaucoup de crime britannique est elucidé par une

*   s   f   r   u   s*

obligatoire éducation technologique du criminel mesestimé. Le

*   y s f   q   u   e*

système fait le fruit rapatrié qui se nant.

"1995 onwards: much of British crime is solved by compulsory technological education of the underrated lawbreaker. The system produces a self-supporting and fruitful repatriation."

OVER the next decade, Britain will evolve into an advanced technological society with many radical approaches to deep seated problems, such as the young persistent lawbreaker.

x	s	n	s	f	r	u	s	y	s	f	q	u	e
c	b	l	o	o	g	c	l	i	l	i	i	i	t
22	18	13	18	6	17	20	18	23	18	6	16	20	5
3	2	11	14	14	7	3	11	1:9	11	1:9	1:9	1:9	19
4	9	4	9	6	8	2	18	5	9	6	7	20	5
3	2	11	5	14	7	3	11	19	11	19	19	10	19
	13	Apr		Jun	28			195	Sep	196	197	2	195
Mar	13		95			24	Nov		Nov			0	
												1	
												0	

During 13 March–13 April 1995, the proposal is made that crime could be drastically reduced by compulsory vocational education. Such a project could include the assessment of an offender's physical and mental health, IQ and educational achievement. Those convicted of a crime would be compelled to undertake vocational courses suited to their needs.

A pilot scheme could be set up between 28 June–24 November 1995.

During September–November 1996, and throughout 1997, evidence grows of a successful turning away of youngsters from crime to a worthwhile career.

Continued monitoring between 1995–2010 demonstrates that young people are being helped into long-term employment in new technological industries, some not yet in existence.

I have concentrated on the young offender in this prediction, but such projects will also be extended to the older and long-term unemployed. Women, especially, will benefit from such a system.

Worldwide innovative education will be a key factor during the next decade, as society realises the potential implications of numerous scientific and technological discoveries.

October 1992 X.89

Women Excel in Law and Business

b

Cinq: de femmes en affaires très excellent à user la technologie
z   d   g   d   r r d
nouvelle. On applique aussi aux poursuites judiciaires là où des
*   d   r   r   c*
essais mettent à les hâter.

"1995 onwards: women in business greatly excel in using new
technology. This also applies to legal proceedings where tests
begin to speed them up."

Aprediction applying to many countries where electronic and computing technology speeds up costly and time-consuming legal and business proceedings.

b	z	d	g	d	r	r	d	d	r	r	c		
i	u	n	q	x	i	l	o	i	n	l	a		
2	24	4	7	4	17	17	4	4	17	17	3		
1:9	20	13	16	22	1:9	11	14	1:9	13	11	1		
2	6	4	7	4	8	8	4	4	8	8	3	=	19
10	20	13	16	4	19	11	5	19	4	2	1	=	7
Feb	6	Apr	11		198		Aug	4	194				197
Oct	0		29	Apr			11	May					
	0												
	2												

Trials could begin during 4 August 1994–11 May 1995. Throughout 1997, it is successfully applied to much social interaction, including legal transactions, within and outside the courts. A lawyer's office could resemble an operating section at NASA! Numerous opportunities will open up for women adapting quickly to these new techniques.

Between 11 April–29 April 1998, technology could revolutionise legal cases in courts that may use video link-ups taking evidence from witnesses at work or home, or even abroad. If a lawyer wishes to cite a previous case as a precedent, the relevant section could be instantly flashed up on the court's video screen. The court could even become 'imaginary', with judge, jury and lawyers never meeting together, but providing 'input' from different locations. (See 'Fibre Optics – Everyone a Space Voyager!')

The prediction then switches to February–October 2006 when women are at the forefront of new technology effecting complex international business transactions at lightning speed.

'Justice' – a woman
– Old Bailey, London   October 1992 II.51

Political Rights for Children

---

y m n
Cinq: l'Europe — droits de pouvoirs politiques d'enfants
n n m p h o
reconnaissent l'esprit curieux d'enfant pendant qu'ils défendent
r r o m r r
sa sécurité. Égalé ses parents, avec futur plus élèvé. Bon jour!

"1995 onwards: Europe — powerful political rights of children recognise the inquiring mind of the child while protecting its safety. Equal to its parents, but with greater potential. A good day!"

A revolution in the status of European children, who acquire rights during 25 April 1995–24 April 1996 that arm them with more control over their relationships with family, school and community. Citizenship and 'tug-of-love' cases could be reviewed.

| y | m | n | n | n | m | p | h | o | r | r | o | m | r | r |
i	d	v	c	x	e	q	i	d	i	a	a	u	s	l
23	12	13	13	13	12	15	8	14	17	17	14	12	17	17
1:9	4	21	3	22	5	16	1:9	4	1:9	1	1	20	18	11
5	12	13	4	4	12	15	8	5	8	8	14	3	8	8
19	4	21	3	22	5	7	19	4	19	1	1	20	9	11
195		25	Apr	Apr	27		198	May 198		Aug	14	3	98	Aug
	Apr	24			27	Jul		Apr		1	Jan	0		Nov
												0		
												2		

Relationships between parents and children will be dramatically altered by new legislation

During 27 April 1998–27 July 1999, a further network of regulations recognises that, with dramatic advances in educational methods predicted, children have become mentally more advanced. Laws could acknowledge their new maturity, while recognising that smaller 'adults' need safeguards. Debate occurs May 1998–April 1999.

During August–November 1998, the legal status of children could be strengthened – a 'good day' for both children and society.

The prediction then jumps to 14 August 2003–1 January 2004 when laws make children equal citizens with their parents, while protectively recognising that children are society's most important future resource. They could vote and make major decisions about their lives, perhaps even electing teenage political representatives. January 1993 IX.36

Men of Europe and America

b   r g r   r p p   r k   r
Cinq: l'homme en société européenne fait une parade d'un futur
p r   s   r   r   f   r   p   r f
sur et fabuleux, pendant qu'homme de l'Amerique gatée devient,
j   s   g
paradoxalement, galets baladeurs.

*"1995 onwards: the man in European society boasts of a fabu-
lous future, while the man of ruined America becomes, paradoxi-
cally, wandering shingle."*

An intriguing contrast is offered by Nostradamus: technology-conscious American men will opt for the natural open-air life. European men will become the scientific 'whiz-kids' of the new age

THE 'ruin' of America is predicted to arise from several geological and ecological disasters occurring within this decade. However, the resilience of the American people to overcome at his massive setback should not be underestimated. A marked upturn in American fortunes is foreseen for 2006 onwards.

From 23–30 October 1996, men of all nations in the European Community will increasingly think of themselves as Europeans first and members of a state second. An event or new law affecting the Community could occur at this time to aid this change in outlook.

By 17 June 1998–18 April 1999, European society will be entering a revolutionary cycle in scientific and technological advancement. New technology could be displayed and celebrated in various ways, probably in connection with exhibitions and events in the run-up to midnight 1999, when the new millennium begins.

In America, meanwhile, during July 1999–May 2000, there could be social migrations across the continent as many American men, affected by the misfortunes predicted for the 1990s, enter a rootless phase and adopt a totally different lifestyle, becoming

b n	r m	g e	r o	r e	p t	p n	r e	k d	r t	p u	r e	s x	r d	r u	f m	r e	p q	r e	f v	j m	s t	g e
2	17	7	17	17	15	15	17	—	17	15	17	18	17	17	6	17	15	17	6	10	18	7
13	12	5	14	5	19	13	5	4	19	20	5	22	4	20	12	5	16	5	21	12	19	5
2	8	7	8	8	6	6	17	—	8	6	17	9	8	8	6	8	15	8	6	10	9	7
13	12	5	5	5	19	13	5	4	19	20	5	22	4	20	3	5	7	5	21	3	19	5

```
Oct     23          196 Jun 17      198  6       26Aug  8    6 Aug      23 Jun 2  199 Jul
        30    Oct         18 Apr          0May 26     0  Mar 5  Jul 26   0      May
                                          0               0              0
                                          2               2              3
```

hoboes and reverting to the pioneer spirit of the Old West. Like so much 'wandering shingle' they could find themselves cast up on many a strange beach. Some may wander the world. More could end up living and working permanently in Europe.

From 26 July 2003–23 June 2004, many new beginnings could blossom in America, until, by 26 August 2006–26 May 2007, Americans could anticipate a dazzling future, buttressed by many technological advances made in Europe in the preceding years.

During 6 August 2008–5 March 2009 America could have recovered greatly from past misfortune and a new generation may begin to rival the European superpower.

February 1993 III.53

Birth Control Cuts World Population

ʃ   x   u ʃ h
Après l'an deux mille la vigueur sort du problème de la
*   c   h   s   t   p   o*
population humaine du monde avec une réussite en
*   r   t   s   r   t   e*
contrôle sophistiqué des naissances. On porte à parachever.

"After the year 2000 vigour departs from the problem of human world population with a success in a sophisticated form of birth control. It is carried to complete."

A story of success in the new millennium against the huge problem of accelerating world population, one that begins with the development of new, advanced techniques of birth control. The possibility of using these techniques first emerges during 14 June 1998–21 April 1999, perhaps with research followed by an early trial, or pilot schemes.

Such is the rate of advance that a wider cross-section of the population could have access to this new application as early as 22 December 2000–11 August 2001. 1 May 2001 is an important date in this process, possibly marking an international conference, or decision.

During 1 January–6 April 2003 the first signs of a fallback in the numbers of births may emerge. From then on, concern in many quarters about the difficulty of controlling world population will ease.

By 4 September 2004, statistics collected throughout the world may confirm a significant drop in numbers of births. During 1 April–17 September 2004, the possibility grows of the birth rate becoming stable in the foreseeable future.

The phrase 'carried to complete' suggests that this new technique may be an advanced form of 'the morning after' pill; supplies could be freely distributed without a doctor's prescription to all women of childbearing age. An alternative may be a form of hormonal skin implant now receiving widespread interest.

Despite religious, moral and, perhaps, some medical pressures, the decision on whether or not to continue a pregnancy will rest with individual women throughout the world.

Apart from the problems currently posed by the accelerating growth of world population, other predictions in this book may also throw light on additional reasons for the introduction of this new technique.

For instance, one prediction states that after the year 2000 genetic techniques of rejuvenation will enable many people to retain their youth and vigour well into old age. Such a development would lend added urgency to the need to curb the rate of increase in births. (See HEALTH: The Old Become Young.) Also, the section titled TRAVEL IN SPACE describes astounding advances in the exploration of our solar system. Part of the motive behind this may lie in the need for human population to expand beyond this planet.

A Vietnamese poster advertising forms of birth control

January 1992 VII.14

f	x	u	f	h	c	h	s	t	p	o	r	t	s	r	t	e
a	a	m	d	l	l	m	d	d	v	n	i	d	a	n	a	a
6	22	20	6	8	3	8	18	19	15	14	17	19	18	17	19	5
1	1	12	4	11	11	12	4	4	21	13	1:9	4	1	13	1	1
6	4	20		8	3	8	9	10	6	14	8	10	9	17	10	5
1	1	3	10	11	11	12	4	4	21	4	19	4	1	4	1	1
6	Apr	2	2	Aug	11		Sep	2	Jun	14	198	2	Sep	17	2	May
Jan	1	0	0	22	Dec		4	0	21	Apr		0	1	Apr	0	1
		0	0					0				0			0	
		3	0					4				4			1	

LEISURE

... where mind and body begin to explore
the freedoms of a new age ...

Fashion Vagabonds

---

a $\int$ a u r u
Peu à peu chroniques de la mode deviennent à perdre le contrôle
u a u r c
sur les vêtements. Les gens sont plus sages. Vagabonds pionniers
y p h
rurals jouent, rient.

"Little by little, fashion journalists come to lose control over clothes. People are more wise. Rural pioneer vagabonds play, laugh."

AN odd prediction highlighting the date 15 April 1998 as the beginning of a happier and more relaxed public mood. Scientific advances may be making life easier for many. Access to entertainment may be demanded of government policies.

One aspect of this scene will relate to fashion. Why fashion journalists should be singled out in this way is not clear, but I suspect that new and amazing advances in the manufacture and appearance of clothes may have something to do with it. By 9 May 2003–7 January 2004, the idea of 'fashion' may be fading, as people acquire greater tolerance of other people's apparel.

Fashion will give way to individual style

Until 13 January 2010, fashion could hold sway over decreasing numbers of people, with choice for many becoming highly individual and often bizarre. Fashion is often perceived as a form of social control, because clothes convey subtle clues about class and status; people with the right 'look' find it easier to gain access to certain desirable groups. This form of 'control' could disappear by 11 August 2010 as everyone gains access to worldwide networks of information, which will hold the real power in the future.

From 11 November 2010–8 August 2011, young pioneers or trend-setters will often resemble old-style country vagabonds, perhaps even adopting breeches and bandanas round their heads. They could wear large hooped earrings and look extremely colourful. Many may adopt a different look every day, dressing up as a favourite character from books, films, or TV. This outrageous period – when the streets of towns and cities could be crowded with lookalikes of famous historical or fictional characters – will appear to hark back nostalgically to the sixties.

To wear something 'different' will no longer arouse criticism. It will be fashionable *not* to follow fashion. Chain stores should take note.

July 1993·III.65

a / e	f / e	a / d	u / v	r / l	u / t	u / t	a / n	u / t	r / s	c / b	y / l	p / n	h / t
1	6	1	20	17	20	20	1	20	17	3	23	15	8
5	5	4	21	11	19	19	13	19	18	2	11	13	19
1	6	1	20	8	20	20	1	2	8	3	5	15	8
5	5	4	3	11	10	10	13	10	9	2	11	4	19
	7	Jan	2	Aug	2	2	Jan	2	Aug	8		15	198
May	9		0	11	0	0	13	0	11	11	Nov	Apr	
			0		1	1		1					
			3		0	0		0					

3-D Epic Films

x   o   m   p   u   P P
Cinq: les films deviennent plus héroiques avec technologie égale
p   b   h o   p o   u   r
à trois dimensions, registré en stéréo. Faut qu'ils rivalisent avec
u   r   s
autres choix pour heure petite.

"1995 onwards: films become more epic, with matching technology in 3-D, recorded in stereo. They must compete with other choices for the brief hour."

THE timescale suggests that, although film-makers will find themselves competing with dazzling new entertainment technologies during the next fifteen years, an entrenched attitude in the industry will prevent the introduction of similar technology, apart from 'tinkering at the edges'. The film industry may go into decline.

During 1994–5, some companies may recognise that films must adapt to new demands. From 29 August–23 July 1996, stereo sound could become an integral part of watching a film, perhaps with headphones attached to cinema seats.

However, by September–October 1998, cinema-going could fall, with the mass market turning to other technologies offering 'direct experience' in their homes (see other predictions in this section). By 2001, the situation may have reached crisis point, with many believing that the glorious era of film-making, as we have known it, is over. Share of the audience could have declined significantly.

Between 2001–2005, the industry could be producing bigger and more expensive epic films. Nevertheless, such will be the competition for the leisured consumer that, from March–August 2001, film-makers could realise that they must compete more aggressively for the 'brief hour'.

An audience watching a 3-D demonstration at the Festival of Britain, 1951

Between 19 July 2010–30 June 2011, film technology will at last catch up, with three-dimensional viewing enabling the viewer to be 'present' in the film.

Part of the film industry's failure to take advantage of new technology could result from America's severe decline, predicted for the middle of this decade. Hollywood could well not be the dominating power in films that it is today.

February 1993 VII.14

x	o	m	p	u	p	p	p	b	h	o	p	o	u	r	u	r	s
i	i	l	q	e	g	g	m	i	n	t	q	i	i	v	a	i	i
22	14	12	15	20	15	15	15	2	8	14	15	14	20	17	20	17	18
1:9	1:9	11	16	5	7	7	12	1:9	13	19	16	1:9	1:9	21	1	1:9	1:9
4	5	12	6	20	15	15	6	2	8	14	15	5	20	8	20	8	9
19	19	11	16	5	7	7	12	10	4	19	7	19	10	3	1	19	10
194	195	12	Jun	2		30	Jun	2	Aug	29		195	2	Aug	2	198	Sep
		Nov	16	0	Jul	19			23	Jul			0	Mar	0		Oct
			0					1					1		0		
			5					0					0		1		

Publishing – Mail Order Revolution

---

g   s   h   d   o
Cinq: une révolution technologique à la vente par
d   x   h   a   e   u   o
correspondance. Par-ci, par-là, les maisons d'édition hument
d   m   a
douteux parfum dur de la cambrousse d'égalité.

"1995 onwards: a technological revolution through mail order. Here and there, publishing houses inhale the harsh, uncertain scent of a country of equality."

---

g q	s n	h i	d q	o v	d n	x i	h p	a l	e n	u i	o n	d f	m o	a t
7	18	8	4	14	4	22	8	1	5	20	14	4	12	1
16	13	1:9	16	21	13	1:9	15	11	13	1:9	13	6	14	19
7	18	8	4	14	4	4	8	1	5	20	14	4	12	10
16	4	19	16	3	4	10	6	11	13	10	4	6	14	10
Jul	18	198	Apr	18		4		9	May	2		18	Dec	2
16	Apr			19	Apr	0	Jun	24		0	Apr	20		0
						0				1				0
						2				0				0

SOPHISTICATED mail order techniques using advertising, catalogues and 'junk mail' offer an enormous range of goods, including books. It follows that organisations with extensive advertising budgets and large stocks of the books being promoted have an in-built advantage. In other words, as in so many other industries, the big boys rule.

However, a revolution in electronics technology begins to impact on the publishing industry between 18 July 1998–16 April 1999. What this means is that publishers will no longer have to print books months in advance to gain sufficient production. Nor will chains of bookshops have to operate huge warehouses to stockpile books. Technology will print, bind and despatch books according to demand.

At present, when orders arrive via a publisher's sales reps or through the post, two things can happen – books confirmed available from stock can be despatched, or, if a book is awaiting production, the bookshop will be informed of the delay.

With new technology, this system could be swept aside. Books will be printed, bound and despatched often on the same day as orders are received. The dominance of big publishers and chains of bookshops will be broken. Small publishers will be able to concentrate on marketing without having their resources drained by production requirements. 'Second-guessing' of likely sales will be a thing of the past.

By 20 April–18 December 2000, the revolution has taken hold – some publishers may find it difficult to work in a system where everyone competes from the same starting-point.

Between 18–19 April 2004, new developments in mail order technology could accentuate the process and by 24 June 2010–May 2011, publishing houses could be using technology capable of producing books at a breathtaking rate.

Will bookshops disappear? For the sake of confirmed browsers like me, I hope not. But the book trade itself could soon change out of all recognition.

Will bookshops still look like this in twenty years' time? Readers may be able to order print-outs of books over the telephone

February 1993 IV.44

Computer Games – The Fabulous World

g   b g   d   b p   r   r p   p

Cinq: le jeux électronique use la technologie à rendre un sens

ƒ   a   k   r   r   r   r ƒ

plus élevé de la réalité entrée par un monde fabuleux, où

   r   ƒ   a ma   s g   a

paradis trompe et l'enfer cache le prix.

"1995 onwards: the computer game uses technology to give a greater sense of reality entered through a fabulous world, where paradise deceives and hell hides the prize."

Virtual Reality in Air Traffic Control, demonstrating its future operation. Optical fibre sensors in the black data glove and the scanner glasses connect him with a computer-generated 3-D image of the airspace he is controlling

g	b	g	d	b	p	r	r	p	p	f	a	k	r	r	r	r	f	r	f	a	m	a	s	g	a
c	e	e	c	e	l	c	e	n	n	l	v		l	e	e	x	o	i	o	e	l	e	e		x
7	2	7	4	2	15	17	17	15	15	6	1	—	17	17	17	17	6	17	6	1	12	1	18	7	1
3	5	5	3	5	11	3	5	13	13	11	21	11	11	5	5	22	14	19	14	5	11	5	5	5	22
7	2	7	4	2	15	8	8	6	6	6	1	—	17	8	8	6	8	6		1	12	1	9	7	1
3	5	5	3	5	11	3	5	4	4	11	3	11	11		10	4	5	19	5	5	11	5	5	5	4

```
      9   7  Apr 2      23 Aug  2   2 Jun 18        Aug 22       198        19  Jan    Jul 1
Mar 5 May 3 0 Nov 8         0   0      25 Nov  2000 4 May    May 21        95  5 Apr
          0             0   0
          5             0   0
```

COMPUTER games have become a huge growth industry, knowing no frontiers. One would think that technology could do no more, but a major breakthrough is predicted from March–1 May 1995. 5 April is an important date in this process.

'Reality entered' strongly hints at a tie-up with Virtual Reality technology. Here, a computerised headset and a sensitised glove enable the user to mentally enter a computer-generated world which holds unlimited possibilities of action, like flying a jet plane, exploring under the sea or going into space. Virtual Reality machines are beginning to appear in amusement arcades and all-night 'raves'. By 1995, they will have become a familiar sight. Linking up Virtual Reality with sophisticated computer games technology could result in the player becoming a 'participant' in his or her own game.

During 19 January–21 May 1998, games may acquire a 'mythological' background populated by ancient 'gods and goddesses', centaurs, dragons and other legendary beasts. The player may be distracted by impressions of paradise, or venture deep into an infernal region to find the object of the game's 'quest'. By this time technology could be conveying very fluid and natural impressions.

In the year 2000, refinements produce an even greater sense of reality, where the player is able to enter a truly 'fabulous world' of imagination and legend.

Such developments would leave the traditional computer game, played on a console, far behind. During 3 May–7 April 2005, such technology could be phased out, just as the long-playing vinyl record has all but disappeared in our own time.

Fibre Optics – Everyone A Space Voyager!

h   r   a   ar   a   d   c   f
Cinq: la fibre optique se joint à la télévision par satellite en
o   a a   f   o   c   a   c   o   a
produire de première main l'expérience de l'espace. Un neuf age
r   a
d'or force cages.

"1995 onwards: fibre optics joins satellite television in producing at first hand the experience of outer space. A new golden era forces open the cages."

h	r	a	a	r	a	d	c	f	o	a	a	f	o	c	a	c	o	a	r	a
i	i	t	e	j	v	p	t	e	i	e	p	i	x	e	p	u	n	e	e	e
8	17	1	1	17	1	4	3	6	14	1	1	6	14	3	1	3	14	1	17	1
1:9	1:9	19	5	10	21	15	19	5	1:9	5	15	1:9	22	5	15	20	13	5	5	5
8	8	1	1	8	1	4	3	6	5	1	1	6	5	3	1	3	5	1	8	1
19	19	10	5	10	3	6	10	5	19	5	6	19	22	5	6	20	4	5		10
198	198	Jan	Jan 8	Jan 13			195		Jan 1	196	May 4				3			Jan	Aug 1	
	2000	May 0		19 May				5 Jun							27	Jun 0		95	2000	
		0														0				
		2														2				

IN the wonderful world of fibre optics one strand of silicon, thinner than a human hair, can carry 20,000 telephone conversations and several hundred TV transmissions. Silicon itself is cheap, but the equipment that receives and transmits signals is expensive. However, as the implications of fibre optics work through the mass leisure market, prices are likely to fall.

What will fibre optics technology do for the viewer?

Imagine that you are sitting at home and you want to watch the F.A. Cup Final at Wembley. Instead of staring at your television screen and watching pictures directed at you by the producer and the camera operators, you don a special headset or computerised goggles.

Immediately, you'll think you are actually *sitting* in the stands, waiting for the referee to blow the first whistle. You'll see everything in 3-D and hear sound in stereo. You won't be restricted to looking in one direction, either. You'll be able to look up at the sky and check the weather, or switch away from the action at one end of the ground to see what the goalkeeper's up to at the other end. In fact, you'll be delightfully fooled into thinking you really are present at any event you're watching.

With fibre optics technology, you'll always have the best seat at the opening ceremony of the Olympic Games, or at the American Superbowl. You could go along with millions of others to a concert by your favourite rock stars. You'll be able to 'book' seats in the stalls for the latest raved-over play or musical in London's theatrical West End or on Broadway. You could watch an opera at La Scala, Milan, or 'visit' the Bolshoi Ballet in Moscow.

I've given only a few examples, but the possibilities are almost limitless for huge numbers of people to share in a range of cultural experiences without ever leaving their homes. Of course, no one can do these things yet, but the technology is coming and it will open up such opportunities to millions of people over the next two decades.

However, the prediction focuses on a single, but dazzling, aspect of this technology – space travel. The section titled TRAVEL IN SPACE contains a series of predictions explaining how we will begin to explore our solar system during the first ten years of the new millennium.

Fibre optics will mentally transport the viewer to any place in the world – or out of it!

These explorations sound immensely exciting, but only a few people will venture into space, compared with the billions left on earth. Films and photos can give us some idea of what it is like to live and work in space, but fibre optics will actually 'beam us up' there so that we'll really feel we are living on a space station, roaming the mountains of the Moon, exploring Mars and Venus, or voyaging through the dark, cold outer reaches of our solar system.

The golden age of fibre optics technology will begin in January 1995. Between 13 January–19 May, satellite television will be involved in setting up a system of participation in real world experiences. Some trials could take place.

During 1 January–5 June 1996, broadcasts could enable people to 'sample' a variety of experiences at first hand.

Gradual at first, from 1998 the process could accelerate so that, by January–1 August 2000, fibre optics transmissions could be a normal aspect of any cultural or sporting event. Freedom from individual isolation will be a key factor. Transmissions to earth from space could be made at this time.

From 4–27 May 2003, a series of spectacular interplanetary broadcasts could enable earthbound people to share mentally and emotionally in the experiences of astronauts.

During January–May 2008, each viewer will have the choice of sharing in the latest and most difficult space voyages to the outer planets.

NATIONS

... while nations cope with changed circumstances ...

America Worn Out by Disaster

---

j   u   z   f
Après l'an deux mille l'Amerique, pays harassé de la grosseur de
    u   v   s   s
désastre, anticipe fatalement un doseur de déséquilibre financier
   s   t   c   s
en échange de stock. Troc.

"After the year 2000, America, a country exhausted by the volume of disaster, inevitably anticipates a measure of financial instability in exchange for stockpiles of goods. Barter."

---

j	u	z	f	u	v	s	s	s	t	o	c	s
i	y	a	e	e	a	q	n	n	n	d	k	c
10	20	24	6	20	21	18	18	18	19	14	3	18
1:9	23	1	5	5	1	16	13	13	13	4	—	3
10	2	6	6	2	3	9	9	9	10	5	3	9
10	5	1	5	5	1	7	4	4	4	4		3
2	2	June	6	2	Mar	9		99	2	May	12	
0	0			0					0			
1	0	1	May	0	1	Jul	Apr	4	0	4		Mar
0	5			5					4			

THE long-lasting and severe economic decline of the United States during the next two decades, here graphically described by Nostradamus, forms the background to all the predictions in this book. It has lasting political and economic consequences for the entire planet.

Nostradamus has already predicted that, during the nineties, America will undergo a series of natural disasters affecting her agricultural and industrial bases.

The Wall Street Crash, 1929. Could it happen to America again?

Consequently, her economic resources become exhausted from 1 March 1997 and her financial system becomes acutely unstable between 1 March 1997–4 April 1999.

The decline continues until 4 March–12 May 2004, when the value of the dollar could fall so sharply that barter – exchange of goods and services instead of money – may become widespread.

America's economic plight could reach its nadir during 1 May–June 2005, with this great nation wholly exhausted by the volume of disaster heaped on her in preceding years.

However, between 2005–2010 the long climb back to stability begins.

September 1991 II.51

Germany and East Europe – Troubles Ease

THIS prediction tells of a gradual easing of the political and economic problems arising from German unification and the collapse of Communism.

---

b   b   f   r   r   q   r
Cinq: l'Allemagne et les pays européens à l'Est deviennent moins

u   u   d   f   r   u   i
inquieter de dilèmmes politiques posés par inégalité sociale.

y   f   q   u
Chomage – c'est un tournant fructueux.

"1995 onwards: Germany and the European countries to the East become less troubled by political problems posed by social inequality. Unemployment – a fruitful turning point."

---

b	b	f	r	r	q	r	u	u	d	f	r	u	i	y	f	q	u
n	g	l	o	l	v	o	n	l	l	p	p	l	l	g	s	o	e
2	2	6	17	17	16	17	20	20	4	6	17	20	1:9	23	6	16	20
13	7	11	14	11	21	14	13	11	11	15	15	11	11	7	18	14	5
2	2	6	17	8	7	8	20	20	4	6	17	20	19	5	6	16	20
4	7	11	5	2	3	5	4	2	11	15	6	2	11	7	9	5	5
2	Feb	23		2	2	Aug	2	2	Apr	23		2		195	Jun	16	2
0		18	May	0	0	May	0	0		26	Jun	0	Nov	7		95	0
0			0	0		0	0			0							0
4			0	0		4	2			2							5

The fall of the Berlin Wall, 1989, which heralded the reunification of Germany

16 June 1995 marks a turning-point in the fortunes of this huge region in central and eastern Europe, with beneficial social change, particularly relating to unemployment, making an impact from 7 November. By the year 2000, former Communist countries to the east of Germany will have done a great deal of 'catching-up' in economic terms with their west European counterparts.

However, in 2002, certain political problems related to inequalities may return. This troubled period could last until 2004, when things quieten down during May–August.

Between 18 May 2004 –23 February 2005, Germany, the economic heart of Europe, will be the focus for an even greater drawing together of European nations.

2005 is a year of fruitful prosperity.

February 1993 X.89

Iran and Jordan in Nuclear Deal

L'Iran — Tehran domestique l'énergie nucléaire, pendant que la
Jordanie le fournit, avec pur uranium miné de son pays. En
guise de pose separé rouvre sol.

"Iran — Tehran harnesses nuclear energy, while Jordan supplies them with pure uranium mined from that country. Instead of an isolated attitude, she opens up her land again."

s i	s i	p q	o t	u i m	s m	g n	u i	s d	s e	c e	h l
18	18	15	14	20	18	7	20	18	18	3	8
1:9	1:9	16	19	1:9	12	13	1:9	4	5	5	11
9	9	6	5	20	9	7	20	9	9	3	8
19	19	7	19	10	3	4	10	4	5	5	2
		Jun 195	2		Sep	7	2		99	Mar	2
199	199	July	0	3	Apr	0		Apr	5	May	0
			1			1					0
			0			0					0

WITH Jordan providing a vital trading link (not necessarily supplying uranium, but bringing other vital goods to this process), Iran learns how to harness nuclear energy, apparently for peaceful purposes, near her capital Tehran.

An important date is 5 April 1999, when her international isolation begins to break down. This thaw continues during May 2000–March 2001 when Iran opens up her land to foreign visitors, possibly even encouraging business and tourism.

Until 3 April–7 September 2010, she will continue to develop nuclear energy using the fission process, a vital element being pure uranium mined, so the prediction indicates, from within her own borders.

During 2010, Iran may begin to switch to the process of nuclear fusion, now used throughout Europe. (See SCIENCE AND TECHNOLOGY.)

Aerial view of Tehran, capital of Iran

January 1991 III.65

China in Revolution – Tibet Freed

> *y   s   s*
> Cinq: frontière juin, or la Chine fusionne la mansuétude à Tibet
> *f   r   s*
> avec cela de sien peuple, lorsqu'un temps approche d'une
> *   s   s   s   r   r   r*
> révolution perpetuelle. Le sort ronge un fondement rose.

> "From 1995 a June frontier, now China merges leniency towards Tibet with that of her own people, as a time of permanent revolution approaches. Life's condition gnaws the rosy foundation."

CHINA invaded Tibet in 1959, causing the country's religious leader, the Dalai Lama, to flee to India. The occupation of Tibet has been oppressive, but, following a general mellowing of policy, Chinese troops may withdraw across the frontier with Tibet after June 1995. The period 5 August 1995–1 February 1996 continues this process.

y	s	s	f	r	s	s	s	s	r	r	r
e	h	l	a	a	e	i	l	l	e	e	o
23	18	18	6	17	18	18	18	18	17	17	17
5	8	11	1	1	5	1:9	11	11	5	5	14
5	9	9	6	8	9	9	9	9	8	8	8
5	8	2	1	1	5	19	2	2	5	5	5
95			96	98		199	9			98	8 Aug
5 Aug		Feb 1		1 May			Feb		Feb 5		2000

In the next two years, internal and external pressure on the Chinese government for democratic reform may cause such a 'revolution' to begin between 1 May (formerly a celebratory day for Communist countries) 1998–9 February 1999. The revolution could be mainly peaceful, but Nostradamus assures us that its effects will be permanent.

The 'rosy foundation' – Marxism diluted by the need to deal with capitalist democracies on an equal basis – will gradually be eroded by the realisation of the Chinese people that their condition will never really change without fundamental democratic reform.

This may finally come about during 8 August 1998–5 February 2000, when many new political structures across the world will be in place for the beginning of the new millennium.

April 1992 IX.36

The Putala's Palace in Chassa. China's long occupation of Tibet is prophesied to end in 1995

The Dome of the Rock, Jerusalem

Arab Nations Occupy Israel

Cinq: après la guerre les nations Arabes seront les sieurs d'Israel

démembré — une voix que pleure. Toutefois, je te parle

judaisme dois sec, futé. Chahut se fache.

"1995 onwards: after the war, the Arab nations will be masters of dismembered Israel — a voice that weeps. Nevertheless, I say to you, Judaism, be dry, crafty. Uproar grows angry."

NOSTRADAMUS has already predicted a war between Israel and her Arab neighbours during 1995–8. This prediction describes the aftermath — Israel defeated, overrun and divided up between her enemies. The Prophet divides the period he is predicting into two — 1994–5 and 2000–2.

z	g	d	d	a	d	l	t	c
e	o	b	q	j	i	u	e	h
24	7	4	4	1	4	11	19	3
5	14	2	16	10	1:9	20	5	8
6	7	4	4	1	4	2	19	3
5	5	2	7	10	19	20	5	8
Jun	7	Apr	4	1	194	2		Mar
	2000	2	Jul	0		0	195	8
				0		0		
				2		2		

At the end of this decade the brave ideal of recreating the nation of Israel, which fell in rebellion against Rome during the first two centuries of the Christian era, will have been crushed in the dirt before thousands of advancing Arab tanks. By 7 June 2000, the Arabs will be masters of Israel, her various regions under the control of several occupying armies.

From 4 April–2 July 2001, the occupation may grow increasingly oppressive and many thousands of Israelis may suffer acute hardship. Little can be done, it appears, to ease the situation. When 'watching' the destiny of Israel, the Jewish character of Nostradamus always identifies completely with her predicament, losing his usual ironic and objective style.

His advice to worldwide Judaism is to prepare for this dreadful event with dry-eyed cunning. 'Don't get emotionally involved' is the message, or it will be impossible to salvage anything from the situation. This period of preparation must begin in 1994 and will last until 2002.

The political 'uproar' signalling the approaching conflict is evident by 8 March 1995.

April 1992 II.51

Refugees Flood France

b   *h*   *b*
Cinq: pour la France, sans doute, telle sotte bourde —

b   *g* *u*   *s*   *t*
immigrants d'Afrique du Nord en même temps que ceux-là qui

b   *u*   *t*   *e*   *p q* *u*
arrivent. Israel, un torrent après la guerre. Prend à bail la sébile.

"1995 onwards: undoubtedly for France, such a foolish mistake — immigrants from North Africa as well as those who arrive. Israel, a torrent after the war. He/she takes out a lease on the begging bowl."

NOSTRADAMUS, French by nationality and Jewish by descent, sees a torrent of misfortune coming from this predicted war, beginning 8 April 1995. The effects on the Middle East and Europe will last well into the new millennium. From July 1996–January 1997, events could turn against Israel and her Arab foes will 'take out a lease' on her territory, occupying it for a number of years.

b	h	b	b	g	u	s	t	b	u	t	e	p	q	u
n	e	d	i	d	n	m	l	n	n	n	r	i	a	i
2	8	2	2	7	20	18	19	2	20	19	5	15	16	20
13	5	4	1:9	4	13	12	11	13	13	13	17	1:9	1	1:9
2	8	2	2	7	20	9	10	2	20	19	5	6	7	20
4	5	4	10	4	4	3	2	4	4	4	8	19	1	10
2	Aug	2	2	Jul	2	Sep	2	Feb	2		195	196	Jul	2
0	May	0	0	Apr	0		0		0					0
0		0	1		0	Mar	0	Apr	0	Apr	8		Jan	1
4		4	0		4		2		4					0

Moslem immigrants praying in Paris

France and other countries will receive Jewish refugees until March–September 2002, when a further influx of Jews and Arabs arrives, perhaps as the result of a new conflict. North Africans fleeing from war and chaos will continue to present huge logistical problems during 2004–10.

Between April 2004–February 2005, immigration continues, with North Africans arriving April–July 2005. During May–August the economic strain tells on France, which will require international aid to cope until 2010.

The raised letters over one part of the prediction spell *buté*, meaning 'inflexible', and this may reflect the intractability of the problem. (See 'General Colin Powell – Vice President'.)

April 1992 I.28

CITIES

... and cities also encounter change ...

Barcelona Outshines Madrid

---

     b   *q*   *y*   *q*
Cinq: l'Espagne magnifique renait la vie, en sus de sa position
        u   *d* *f*   *y*   *P*
aussi tête culturelle en l'Europe. Mérite est axé sur Barcelona.
 m   *f*   *q*
Madrid — c'est humilié, terne, infructueux.

"1995 onwards: Magnificent Spain gains a new lease of life adding to her position as cultural leader of Europe Her worth is centred on Barcelona. Humiliated Madrid is lifeless, sterile."

---

b	q	y	q	u	d	f	y	p	m	f	q
l	g	i	v	l	l	p	e	l	a	l	x
2	16	23	16	20	4	6	23	15	12	6	16
11	7	1:9	21	11	11	15	5	11	1	11	22
2	7	5	7	2	4	6	5	6	3	6	7
2	7	19	3	2	2	6	5	2	1	2	4
Feb	7	195	0	2		Oct	May 22				
			0								
2	July		0	Apr		6					2004
			2								

HARSH words for Madrid — indeed, Nostradamus appears to say that Barcelona — as well as becoming its cultural centre — may become the political capital of Spain.

The dating spans nine years from 1995. By the beginning of that year, Spain has already blossomed into the cultural centre of Europe, reaching an intense peak of activity between 7 February–2 July.

During the next five years, Barcelona, site of the 1992 Olympic Games, grows in stature until it becomes the foremost Spanish city during 2 October 2000 – 6 April 2001.

By 22 May 2004, Madrid has become a political and cultural backwater.

The Sagrada Famiglia, Barcelona

January 1992 X.89

Johannesburg Renamed

---

      z   *f*   *v*   *x*

Cinq: Afrique du Sud — le peuple noir renomme Johannesburg.

    t   *d*   *l*   *d*   *t*

Amasse hate, un coup fatal à sagesse. Les sieurs précédents

    p *i*   *s*   *t*   *s*

croient que cela ne sert à rien de daigner.

"1995 onwards: South Africa — the black people rename Johannesburg. They pile up haste, fatal blow to wisdom. The former masters believe that it is useless to deign."

THE prediction indicates that between 11 September 1996–24 April 1997, South Africa will experience great difficulties over the integration of her peoples after the long era of apartheid.

| z | f | v | x | t | d | l | d | t | p | i | s | t | s |
q	p	e	u	a	n	p	g	n	n	q	n	n	n
24	6	21	22	19	4	11	4	19	15	11	18	19	18
16	15	5	20	1	13	15	7	13	13	16	13	13	13
6	6	21	4	10	4	11	4	19	6	11	9	19	9
16	6	5	20	1	13	15	7	4	4	7	13	4	13
Jun	27		4	2	Apr	15			196	11	Sep		199
	22	May	0	0		28	Jul	Apr	24			Apr	13
			0	0									
			2	1									

The former white rulers will come to believe that 'it is useless to deign' (13 April 1999). The use of 'deign' or 'condescend' suggests that their attitude to the new reforms is one of the main problems. They cannot be whole-hearted in their support. Resentment could produce a resistance that is prolonged and occasionally violent.

During 28 July 2001–15 April 2002, hasty and ill-conceived decisions all add up to a fatal mistake.

The outcome is decisive with black South African citizens asserting themselves in adopting an African name for the capital Johannesburg, and possibly one for South Africa as well (27 June 2004–22 May 2005).

December 1991 II.51

Johannesburg: Soweto and city skyline

London Threatened by Floods

---

b $\quad$ x $\quad$ b $\qquad$ p $\quad$ h $\quad$ r $\quad$ p $\quad$ p $\qquad$ h

Cinq: au Royaume-Uni Londres pincé de la peur d'une déluge.

r $\qquad$ p $\quad$ r $\qquad$ r $\qquad$ r

La terre de remblai de la Tamise fortifiante jusqu'à Kent. Gué

p $\quad$ r $\quad$ f $\qquad$ a

flageolé fatigue transports routiers.

"1995 onwards: in the United Kingdom London is gripped by fear of flooding. The Thames embankment strengthened as far as Kent. A ford that gives way imposes a strain on road transport."

MUCH of this prediction is directed towards 1998. During the decade, London becomes gripped by a fear of potentially disastrous flooding in the city. This anxiety lasts until at least 6 May 1998, but may be increased by events during 20 August 1998–9 May 1999.

The Thames Flood Barrier in London

b	x	b	p	h	r	p	p	h	r	p	r	r	r	p	r	f	a
i	u	y	o	i	l	e	u	e	t	e	d	i	t	l	i	t	o
2	22	2	15	8	17	15	15	8	17	15	17	17	17	15	17	6	1
1:9	20	23	14	1:9	11	5	20	5	19	5	4	1:9	19	11	1:9	19	14
2	4	2	6	8	8	6	6	8	8	6	8	8	8	6	8	6	1
10	2	5	5	19	2	5	2	5	19	5	4	19	19	2	19	19	5
2	Apr	Feb	6	198	Aug	20		198		Jun	8	198	198	6	198	196	1
0	Feb	5	May				9 May			5	Apr			Feb			May
1																	
0																	

The river Thames runs along the northern border of the county of Kent. So widespread is the concern that its embankments will be reinforced as far as Kent to prevent the river overflowing its banks, a significant period being 8 June 1998–5 April 1999.

The 'ford' or bridge that threatens to give way over a period may cause major disruption to commuter traffic flowing into London, perhaps from the south-east. Signs of structural fatigue could begin to show from 1 May 1996 and may possibly be connected with the expected rise in traffic resulting from the opening of the Channel Tunnel (see 'The Channel Tunnel'). This problem will last until 1998, a significant date being 6 February.

Until, or during, February–April 2010, other areas of Britain may also be affected by serious flooding.

February 1992 III.53

Moscow Exhibits Nazi Loot

h   a   a   a   f   o   b   a   l

Cinq: le cité de Moscou devient un centre pour l'exposition du

a   f   o   c   a   c   o   q   a

larcin des Nazis. La France proteste, mais le désir de l'argent

r   a

rafferme agrandir.

"1995 onwards: the city of Moscow becomes a centre for the exhibition of booty stolen by the Nazis. France protests, but the desire for money strengthens expansion."

h	a	a	a	f	o	b	a	l	a	f	o	c	a	c	o	q	a	r	a
i	t	e	s	v	n	t	x	u	n	s	z	n	t	i	i	d	t	m	d
8	1	1	1	6	14	2	1	11	1	6	14	3	1	3	14	16	1	17	1
1:9	19	5	18	21	13	19	22	20	13	18	24	13	19	1:9	1:9	4	19	12	4
8	1	1	1	6	14	2	1	2	1	6	5	3	1	3	5	16	1	8	10
19	19	5	9	3	4	10	4	20	4	9	6	3	10	10	19	4	10	12	4
198	Jan 1		Jan 23			2	Jan 96		May 7					195				17 Aug	2
	195		26 Apr			0	Apr					19 Oct				Apr 22			0
						0													0
						2													4

IN 1945, at the end of the Second World War, Germany was overrun by Allied forces, including Soviet troops coming from the east. During the years of its occupation the Nazi regime had looted thousands of fabulous art treasures from private collections, art galleries and museums all over Europe. Much of this treasure was still stored in Germany. It was transferred to Russia and stored in secret vaults and archives controlled by the Kremlin and the KGB in Moscow, where it remained until the collapse of the Soviet Union at the end of 1991.

Since the emergence of Russia as a powerful, independent state, many stories about the huge collection of Nazi spoils still in Moscow have begun to surface.

The prediction states that from 1 January 1995 the Moscow city authorities could decide to exhibit some of these treasures, as an instant draw for foreign tourists.

During 7 May–19 October, there could be a bitter international row with France, since she will claim that many of these items were originally stolen from French public and private collections. However, they will not be returned, because the exhibition is attracting badly needed foreign currency for the city.

During January–April 1996, Moscow could be accused of benefiting from theft, but the city may continue to bring out more and more exhibits from its vaults. By 1998, many hundreds or thousands of items looted by the Nazis could be on display, including treasures believed lost for ever.

During 23 January–26 April 2002, Moscow may well have become a world centre for the arts. The city's need for money is still urgent and between 22 April–17 August 2004, a programme of expansion in museums and galleries could be accelerated.

L'argent also means 'silver'. A particular argument over the exhibition of valuable silverware could break out.

Art treasures confiscated by the Nazis were eventually recaptured by Allied troops at the end of the Second World War. However, many disappeared from East Germany after it was occupied by Soviet forces

February 1993 VIII.4

New York – Magnet for the Destitute

Cinq: en l'Amérique le cité de New York rallie la population.
Sera une base pour soigner les abaissés. Un amant dur au jugé
trébuche, fatigué, frappé par drogués.

"1995 onwards: in America the city of New York rallies the
people. It will be a base for looking after the downtrodden. A
lover by guesswork, it stumbles, tired, attacked by drug addicts."

p	d	x	d	h	f	r	r	r	r	f	f	p	r	f	m	t
i	c	y	e	u	s	u	s	o	l	i	u	u	i	e	a	o
15	4	22	4	8	6	17	17	17	17	6	6	15	17	6	12	19
1:9	3	23	5	20	18	20	18	14	11	1:9	20	20	1:9	5	1	14
6	4	4	4	8	6	8	8	8	8	6	6	6	8	6	3	19
19	3	5	5	2	9	2	9	5	2	19	2	2	19	5	1	4
196			8 Apr	Aug 14			98	Aug 8	196		Jun 6	198		6	Mar	
	Mar 10		2		Nov		5 Feb			2 Feb			May 1	194		

BETWEEN 1 May 1994–6 March 1995, the drug problem in New York reaches unparalleled heights, to be worsened by enormous numbers of unemployed, homeless people pouring in from other states as a result of severe economic depression. Beginning in 1996, measures will be taken by the city authorities to deal with this overwhelming logistical problem.

At first, during 8 April 1996–10 March 1997, these measures look like succeeding, particularly during 8 August–5 February. However, the city's success ensures it becomes a magnet for more and more people in distress during 14 August 1998–2 November 1999.

The official system cracks up. Voluntary organisations, trying to make caring decisions without city back-up or the necessary expertise, become exhausted during 6 June 1998–2 February 1999.

Total breakdown of the welfare system seems likely.

WORLD PEOPLE

... when the famous may walk over strange ground ...

Boris Becker Wins Film Role

u   *g* *g*   *d*   *p*

Cinq: Boris Becker d'Allemagne — une part prise en film propre

    h   *a*   *r*

autour de la chute du Mur à Berlin, parce que le tennis

 r   *r* *r* *f* *j* *g*   *a*

n'intéresse plus. Un faux pas. Déclare forfait.

"*1995 onwards: Boris Becker of Germany — a part taken in a suitable film about the fall of the Berlin Wall, because tennis no longer interests. A wrong move. He withdraws.*"

u c	g n	g u	d e	p e	h c	a c	r i	r i	r l	r n	f u	j s	g l	a i
20	7	7	4	15	8	1	17	17	17	17	6	10	7	1
3	13	20	5	5	3	3	1:9	1:9	11	13	20	18	11	1:9
20	7	7	4	6	8	1	8	8	8	8	6	10	7	1
3	4	20	5	5	3	3	19	19	2	4	20	9	2	19=10
2007	97		Jun	9			198	198	8	8	6	2	Jul	2
Mar 4		2000		8	Mar				Feb	Apr				
											0	0	2	0
											2	9		0

THIS prediction looks far ahead into Boris Becker's future – indicating that he may eventually represent Germany in more ways than as a tennis professional.

One such opportunity arises in a film role offered to him between 1997–2000. The film, an appropriate story about the fall of the Berlin Wall, will be produced during those three years.

By 8 February 1998, tennis will not interest Becker as it did before. By this time he will be about thirty and probably casting around for alternative careers, often a difficult area for tennis players with an illustrious history. Becker won Wimbledon at the age of seventeen and has never been out of the headlines since.

At first, the film, possibly made during 9 June 1998–8 March 1999, will offer an attractive career. Nevertheless, he could decide to withdraw from future acting commitments around 2 July 2000.

However, the next important date in his life is 8 April 2006, when he appears to have made 'a wrong move', or mistake, which is publicly acknowledged.

An alternative reading for the last two dates is that between 7 February 2001–8 April 2006, he may take up acting full-time and *then* retire, having decided it is not the career he wants.

The final date – 4 March 2007 – springs from the linking of his name and country. I cannot help feeling that this may signify either a straightforward political career, or a post representing his country at a high level.

Since the dating ends here, he may at last have found his true 'role' in life. In the meantime, his retirement from tennis will only bring his many other talents into public view.

Boris Becker assumes some dramatic poses, but will a film career satisfy his ambition?

June 1992 III.53

Branagh, Thompson – Separate Careers

r p   h   e   t   e   p   l   f l

Cinq: on voit la star anglaise Emma Thompson en une série de

p   p   l   o   p o   r   u

films dramatiques qu'ont du succès. Son mari Kenneth Branagh

e   e   r e   s

se prouve avec deux productions aux théâtres.

"*1995 onwards: the English star Emma Thompson is seen in a series of dramatic and successful films. Her husband, Kenneth Branagh, proves himself with two theatrical productions.*"

**Kenneth Branagh and
Emma Thompson**

r	p	h	e	t	e	p	l	f	l	p	p	l	o	p	o	r	u	e	e	r	e	s
q	n	a	a	a	m	m	n	i	d	m	a	q	d	n	m	–	g	a	d	n	a	a
17	15	8	5	19	5	15	11	6	11	15	15	11	14	15	14	17	20	5	5	17	5	18
16	13	1	1	1	12	12	13	1:9	4	12	1	16	4	13	12	–	7	1	4	13	1	1
17	6	8	5	10	5	15	11	6	11		15	11		6	5	17	20	5	5	17	5	9
7	13	1	1	1	12	12	4	19	4	9	1	7	9	4	12		7	1	4	4	1	1
		31May	2		May	26		196		Nov		15 Nov			2	May17	2		May22		95	
			0			24 Apr		94				Jan 97			0	Dec	0		5 Apr	1	Jan	
			0												0		0					
			1												0		7					

EMMA Thompson, who at the time of writing (February 1993) has received an Oscar nomination for her role in the film *Howards End*, is predicted to go on to a major film career. Her husband, Kenneth Branagh, with a glittering career in classical theatre already behind him, plus a hit Hollywood film *Dead Again*, will head a major theatrical project during the nineties.

By November 1994, Emma Thompson could be in great demand by film directors, while from 1 January 1995, Kenneth Branagh may be heavily involved in theatrical ventures. The date 1 January 1995 suggests that he could have accepted a post to become the director of either an existing theatrical institution or a new organisation.

By 26 May 1996–24 April 1997, Emma Thompson will be making a series of dramatic films that experience great success by January–15 November 1997. The latter date suggests a royal première.

During December 2000–17 May 2001, Kenneth Branagh may be making world headlines. Between 15 July 2001–31 May 2001, the emphasis is on England, perhaps in both films and theatre. The prediction then jumps to 5 April–22 May 2007, when Branagh achieves an even greater breakthrough with two famous productions.

The timescale suggests that the theatrical project which Branagh takes up from 1 January 1995 could be connected with cultural celebrations for the year 2000.

February 1993 VII14

Note: Emma Thompson won the 1993 Oscar for Best Actress.

Richard Branson – Airline Policy Targets Women

   q   **b**   **P**   **b**   **q**

Cinq: l'entrepreneur Richard Branson, au but de faire tête

             b   **s**   **b** **q**   **u**

suprême sa compagnie d'aviation, table sur l'audace géniale par

    l   **m l**   **l**   **q**   **u**

le truchement d'un gros effort aux touristes seules.

"The entrepreneur Richard Branson, intending to make his air-line the leader in the field, counts on inspired audacity with the aid of a great effort solely towards women tourists."

FORMER boss of Virgin Records, Richard Branson is far-sighted enough to know that you do not run an international airline like Virgin by standing still. Great social changes are on the way. By the end of the decade, women working in new technologies will be a source of economic power.

q n	b n	p c	b n	q i	b n	s n	b c	q n	u a	l h	m d	l n	l f	q a	u i
16	2	15	2	16	2	18	2	16	20	11	12	11	11	16	20
13	13	3	13	1:9	13	13	3	13	1	8	4	13	6	1	1:9
7	2	15	2	7	2	18	2	7	20	11	12	2	2	7	20
13	13	3	4	19	4	3	3	13	1	8	4	13	6	1	10
July	19			197			22	Jul	2				27	Jul	2
		29	Apr		Apr	19			0	Aug	24				0
									0						1
									1						0

Richard Branson celebrating Virgin's maiden voyage

By 19 July 1997–29 April 1998, Richard Branson could be contemplating radical developments in airline policy to edge Virgin ahead of its other rivals.

During 19 April–22 July 2001, Virgin could adopt a series of dramatic and inspired policy moves aimed at fundamental changes affecting the status and spending power of women, beginning to make an impact at this time. Special travel offers tailored to suit women tourists travelling alone, in groups, or with their families, could be targeted on this important new market.

By 24 August 2010–27 July 2011, many tourist organisations will have realised that women demand a new response from the service and leisure industries. Those following tradition could fall by the wayside, but Virgin with its forward looking policies may well have got off the ground first.

February 1993 I.28

Cher – A Torch of Compassion

      x   *v*   *g*

Cinq: la chanteuse Américaine, Cher, allume une torche pour ses

f   *P*   *P*

compatriotes. Répond souvent au S.O.S. par entrer les rues. Elle

h *p* *r h*   *p*   *o*   *v*   *e*

aide ceux-là qui se blottent, froids, sans un sou.

"1995 onwards: the American singer, Cher, lights a torch for her compatriots. She often answers an S.O.S. by going into the streets. She helps those who huddle up, cold, penniless."

| x | v | g | f | p | p | h | p | r | h | p | o | v | e |
n	m	l	c	a	a	a	c	a	q	l	d	a	n
22	21	7	6	15	15	8	15	17	8	15	14	21	5
13	12	11	3	1	1	1	3	1	16	11	4	1	13
4	3	7	6	6	6	8	6	8	8	6	5	3	5
4	3	2	3	1	1	1	3	1	7	2	4	1	4
Apr	2000		96	Jun	98				98	6	May	Mar	
	7	Feb		Jan	1	Jan			Jul	6		2000	

DURING bleak years for many Americans left destitute by economic and natural catastrophe, the American singer and actress Cher becomes a beacon of compassion with her charitable work among the homeless. Activity in this area is sparked off from January 1996.

The work will stretch her capabilities up to the year 2000.

By June 1998–1 January 1999, she may be involved in an organisation or network active day and night on the streets among thousands of people, giving out blankets and food. During 6 May–6 July, she could be offering particular aid to huddled, cold groups, perhaps living with them for a time.

This work will take up much time that would normally be spent on recording or acting, so that by March 2000 Cher herself could be financially worse off.

Nevertheless, her example will light the way for many other friends and contacts in American show business to get involved in this work, particularly during April 2000–7 February 2001.

Cher, who will devote her energies and money to charitable work

June 1992 VII.14

Michael Douglas — Strong Oak in Catastrophe

d   n   r   a   a
Cinq; Michael Douglas, le chêne fort en catastrophe de

f   r   o   n   a
l'Amérique, où organise d'arrache-pied en paralysie officielle.

s   r   a
Force obstacle à l'écart.

"1995 onwards: Michael Douglas, the strong oak in America's catastrophe, where he organises relentlessly in official paralysis. He forces the obstacle aside."

| d | n | r | a | a | f | r | o | n | a | s | r | a |
c	e	h	t	h	e	s	h	y	i	l	l	t
4	13	17	1	1	6	17	14	13	1	18	17	1
3	5	8	19	8	5	18	8	23	1:9	11	11	19
4	4	8	10	1	6	8	5	4	10	9	8	10
3	5	8	10	8	5	18	8	5	10	2	2	10
Apr	12		0		96		Aug	95	0	Sep	Aug	0
	8	Aug	0		May	18	Aug		0	Feb	Feb	0
			0									0
			2							2		2

MICHAEL Douglas, immensely successful film actor, producer and son of an equally famous father, Kirk Douglas, will become the strong man of America in her hour of need.

His most challenging and fulfilling role could begin to make itself known to him with all America in a state of social chaos,

following predicted natural and economic catastrophe in California and elsewhere.

Hundreds of thousands of people could become homeless and destitute.

Government and bureaucracy can only function in relative stability, but these unprecedented conditions, comparable only to a state of invasion, or civil war, will produce complete 'official paralysis'. The system will be in shock.

Douglas and others like him will have to do their own organising and he performs this task 'relentlessly', particularly from 18 August 1995, involving himself with creating a social structure which will provide order and care within the community.

From May 1996, he may take on government itself, producing radical short cuts through apparently impossible problems and coming up against official opposition as a result. His work will certainly extend to many areas.

This period will last until the year 2000 when he takes on a central 'strong man' responsibility, possibly in the American government itself, a role dominant during August 2000–February 2001.

Michael Douglas, whose leadership qualities may lead him into government

June 1992 VIII.4

Hopkins to Play Hannibal in Europe

   x   *x*   *v*   *g*   *s*   *v*   *s*   *t*
Cinq: encore on attribue à l'acteur Anthony Hopkins le rôle de
   s   *h*   *h*   *s*   *s*   *p*   *o*
Hannibal Lector, mais on met le film en Europe parce que
     u s   *v t*   *e*   *s*
Californie ne peut pas le produire. Pur succès su.

"*1995 onwards: the actor Anthony Hopkins is again cast in the role of Hannibal Lecter, but the film is directed in Europe because California cannot produce it. Pure success known.*"

IN 1992, Anthony Hopkins won a Hollywood Oscar as Best Actor for portraying the terrifying cannibal psychologist Hannibal Lecter in *The Silence of the Lambs*. The film also collected another four Oscars.

x	x	v	g	s	v	s	t	s	h	h	s	s	p	o	u	s	v	t	e	s
n	c	a	a	c	y	k	l	b	a	n	m	n	a	q	i	n	a	l	i	c
22	22	21	7	18	21	18	19	18	8	8	18	18	15	14	20	18	21	19	5	18
13	3	1	1	3	23	−	11	2	1	13	12	13	1	16	1:9	13	1	11	1:9	3
4	4	3	7	9	3	9	19	9	8	8	9	9	6	5	20	9	3	10	5	9
4	3	1	1	3	5	−	2	2	1	4	3	4	1	7	10	4	1	2	10	3
Apr	7		97		3	Sep		199	Aug	98			96	May	2	9	Mar	2	May	9
			9	Mar	May	4			5	Mar			Apr	1	Jul	0	Apr	1	0	2003
															1				0	
															0				2	

Anthony Hopkins, who will play Hannibal Lector again in a sequel to *Silence of the Lambs* made in Europe

Despite his comments in March 1993, the prediction tells us that Hopkins will play Lector again – but this time the film will be made in Europe, because 'California cannot produce it'. Nostradamus has predicted earthquake disaster for California, including Hollywood, in this decade.

The prediction begins on 1 April 1996, when the European film industry, including Britain, will be much more powerful than today. A project to film the sequel may take shape. During 7 April 1997–10 March 1998, Hopkins will accept the role after lengthy negotiations. The film will be made during August 1998–5 March 1999 and probably go on general release between 4 May–3 September 1999.

The prediction then leaps to 2002, when the American film industry may be attempting to make a third film starring Hopkins as Lector during 1 April–9 March 2003, but the project could fail by 9 May.

However, California could be making real strides in recovering her former status in the film industry by July 2010–May 2011.

June 1992 VII.14

Lineker Trains Young Footballers

r u x   p h p h f   a
Cinq: Gary Lineker parait une dernière fois avant abandonner
p   u f   p   t
le football comme joueur. Entreprend d'enseigner flasque gars —
s u   g
l'arbre mûr dans une pepinière.

"1995 onwards: Gary Lineker appears one last time before leaving football as a player. He sets out to teach the flabby lad — a mature tree in a nursery of trees."

r	u	x	p	h	p	h	f	a	p	u	f	p	t	s	u	g
n	y	e	i	e	n	i	v	e	e	o	o	n	n	n	n	i
17	20	22	15	8	15	8	6	1	15	20	6	15	19	18	20	7
13	23	5	1:9	5	13	1:9	21	5	5	14	14	13	13	13	13	1:9
8	2	4	6	8	6	8	6	1	6	2	6	6	19	9	2	7
4	5	5	19	5	4	19	3	5	5	5	5	4	4	4	4	19
Oct	4		196	Aug	6	198		July	2		June	2		Sep	2	197
4		Oct	5	Apr				95	5	May		5	0			
												0		194	4	Apr
												0				

G ARY Lineker has had a hugely successful career as a professional footballer and is one of the most popular and respected men in the game. In his mid-thirties, when this prediction begins, he will be thinking seriously about an alternative career. Although he has said he would like to become a football manager, an unexpected, challenging opportunity opens up for him at this point.

During 4 September 1994–2 April 1997, Lineker may become increasingly involved with a National Football Training School for youngsters who show exceptional talent. Such a school would combine a normal educational day with physical training and specialist coaching. Lineker's character and skills would make him ideally suited to take charge of the training and coaching programme.

During 5 May–2 July 1995, he may make a decision to commit himself full-time to the project and the period 4 October 1996–4 October 1997 could mark his last year as a full-time player.

It is possible that he will return to football temporarily during 6 August 1998–5 April 1999, either playing or as a manager, but the prediction indicates that by 5 June 2000 he is again fully involved with the national programme.

... and training on the field

June 1992 III.53

Madonna – A Breakdown

AROUND 6 February 1995, the American singer Madonna may experience a severe depression, coming close to a breakdown. This experience could last for several months, but it appears that on 5 August in that year she will make a live international TV broadcast, perhaps appealing for aid to stricken communities in America.

   b   *x*   *l*   *d*
Cinq: la chanteuse américaine, Madonna, à coup futé, fait

  l   *h*   *d*   *s* *s*   *l* *s r* *s*
fréquents voyages à Londres où parvient au zénith. Un jour, en

       s   *e*   *r*   *'s*
direct, pleure désemparée. Dit: 'les gens lésés'.

"1995 onwards: the American singer, Madonna, in a smart move, makes frequent trips to London where she reaches the zenith. One day, live, she is distraught and crying. She speaks of 'the injured people'."

b	x	l	d	l	h	d	s	s	l	s	r	s	s	e	r	s
n	n	n	a	q	y	n	v	a	h	n	o	n	u	p	i	n
2	22	11	4	11	8	4	18	18	11	18	17	18	18	5	17	18
13	13	13	1	16	23	13	21	1	8	13	14	14	20	15	1:9	13
2	4	2	4	2	8	4	9	9	2	9	8	9	9	5	8	9
4	4	4	1	7	5	4	3	1	8	4	5	5	2	6	19	4
2	Apr	2004		2000		4 Sep		2	0 Sep		Aug		95	198	9	
0	4	Apr 1		Jul 5		Apr 3		0	0 Apr		5	95	Feb 6		Apr	
0								0	0							
4								0	2							

On 9 April 1998, she may make another appeal for 'the injured people' of America, or she could go on a tour of personal appearances and speeches, drumming up aid.

During the year 2000, she may begin making frequent journeys to London (3 April–5 July–4 September) in order to promote her career in the growing European market. Her European appearances could reach a peak of activity during September 2000–April 2001 and may be connected with celebrations for the new millennium.

Around April 2004 she may decide that adoption of British nationality could amount to a smart career move.

Image-conscious Madonna may yet surprise her audiences with an unexpected career move in the new millennium

June 1992 II.51

General Colin Powell – Vice-President

o   m   s   m d   o   d   o
Cinq: général américain, Colin Powell, devient vice-président à
d   x   u   o   r   u o   d   a
chef George Bush après le début de guerre au Moyen-Orient.
m   a   o
Haut Saddam Hussein capte la paix.

"1995 onwards: American general, Colin Powell, becomes Vice-President to the leader George Bush after the outbreak of war in the Middle East. Disdainful Saddam Hussein captures the peace."

General Colin Powell salutes the colour of The 1st Battalion Grenadier Guards

IN 1991, I published a series of predictions, one of which indicated that President George Bush would only win a second term of office with a vice-presidential candidate other than Dan Quayle. In the event, Bush kept Quayle as his running-mate and went down to defeat at the hands of a relatively unknown Governor from Arkansas, Bill Clinton.

The question then was – had the prediction failed? In my experience these predictions all come true eventually. It seemed to me that the answer lay in the identification of this unknown Vice-President, whoever he or she might be.

Prophecies of a war in the Middle East were also published in 1991 and several predictions in this book continue that theme. At the heart of the conflict will be a name the West knows well – Saddam Hussein. With such a scenario, it might be thought good sense to elect to the presidency and vice-presidency two men who had fought against Saddam before – his old adversaries George Bush and former Chief of Staff, Colin Powell.

o	m	s	m	d	o	d	o	d	x	u	o	r	u	o	d	a	m	a	o
q	n	n	i	p	i	v	i	f	e	e	e	b	e	g	y	n	i	e	i
14	12	18	12	4	14	4	4	4	22	20	14	17	20	14	4	4	12	1	14
16	13	13	1:9	15	1:9	21	1:9	6	5	5	5	2	5	7	23	13	1:9	5	1:9
5	3	9	12	4	5	4	4	4	4	20	14	8	20	5	4	4	3	1	5
7	4	4	10	6	19	3	19	6	5	5	5	2	5	7	23	4	10	5	19

May 28				195		Apr 8			Apr 2	14	Aug 2		May 8			3		Jan 195	
	25 Jun					Mar	196		May 0		May 2	0			30		Apr 0	May	
									0			0					0		
									5			5					2		

During 28 May–25 June 1995, Colin Powell could let it be known that he will run for political office during 1996. Negotiations with George Bush's advisers could take place at this point. Much urgency and alarm will be in the air as, during January–May 1995, Saddam Hussein will have moved against Israel to 'capture the peace', perhaps breaking a peace treaty between the Arab States and Israel. Other predictions state that Israel will be defeated and occupied by an Arab alliance. (See 'Arab Nations Occupy Israel'.)

During 8 April 1996–March 1997, Colin Powell may be elected the first black Vice-President of the United States, distinguishing himself early on in this role.

At this point there is no indication that America will intervene militarily, but she might act to prevent the conflict spreading beyond the Middle East.

Powell may well follow George Bush into the presidency in the year 2000. Conflict with Saddam Hussein during 8 May 2003–30 April 2004 is possible.

However, during May 2005–April 2006, and particularly between 2 May–14 August 2005, Powell could be engaged in restoring the American economy to its former strength. By this time he would be in his second term.

**America's first
black President?**

The phrase 'captures the peace' could be shorthand for the holy places of 'The Prince of Peace' or Christendom in Israel. Their destruction could be the subject of the last of the three prophecies of Fatima, revealed in visions to a group of children in 1917. Popes throughout this century have refused to make the third prophecy public. Perhaps the conflict in the early years of the century is a new Crusade to liberate these places of veneration.   February 1993 IV.44

Spielberg Revives British Film Industry

   p   *b*   *h*   *b*   *s*   *b s*

Cinq: Steven Spielberg brave l'Amérique, un rogue rustre, et fait

     s   *x*   *s*   *b*

un pont que drague la molle industrie britannique de film au

        r   *m*   *r*   *p*   *i*

cadre. Satisfait à toute l'Europe avec telle queue d'or.

"*1995 onwards: Steven Spielberg defies America, an arrogant lout, and makes a bridge that drags the feeble British film industry into the frame. It satisfies all Europe with such a golden queue.*"

The phenomenally successful film director Steven Spielberg – predicted to bring his Midas touch to the British film industry

H ARSH words from Nostradamus for the attitude of the American film industry, reflecting a protectionist mood in difficult times.

Conversely, the British film industry, always struggling for backing, may enter a golden and profitable era of film-making during 1996–2004.

p	b	h	b	s	b	s	s	x	s	b	r	m	r	p	i
n	i	v	i	n	e	f	n	i	i	i	i	u	v	t	d
15	2	8	2	18	2	18	18	22	18	2	17	12	17	15	1:9
13	1:9	21	1:9	13	5	6	13	1:9	1:9	1:9	1:9	20	21	19	4
6	2	8	2	18	2	9	9	4	9	2	8	3	8	6	10
4	19	3	19	4	5	6	4	10	19	10	19	20	3	19	4
2	Feb			28	Feb		Sep	4	199	2	198	3	8	196	2
0	19	Mar	28		96		4	Oct		Oct		3	Mar		0
0												0			0
0												2			4

166

At the heart of this renaissance will be the American director Steven Spielberg who has made some of the most popular films in the history of cinema, including *Jaws*, *Close Encounters of the Third Kind*, *ET* and the *Indiana Jones* trilogy. Spielberg has always admired British films, virtually non-existent at the beginning of the nineties, but his new project to revitalise the industry is not a charitable gesture. 'In the frame' is the huge European mass market now forming from the ever-expanding EC and former Communist countries.

Opposition to his plans could arise among fellow American film-makers during 28 March 1996–28 February 1997. Hollywood is predicted to be suffering a severe decline at this time and the feeling may be that Spielberg ought to direct his talents there.

Spielberg may direct a film, or a series of films, using British technical expertise and British actors which, by 2 October 1998, proves a stunning success. This era is a 'bridge', enabling the British industry to cross towards a brilliant era (4 September–4 October 1999).

Between 19 February 2000–8 March 2003, Spielberg may be involved in cultural celebrations of the new millennium, but on the horizon for him is a growing film 'empire' throughout Europe.

February 1992 I.28

Andrew Lloyd Webber Aids American Arts

Cinq: le compositeur britannique Andrew Lloyd Webber y
devient chef d'un groupe fié que réorganise l'aide financière sans
taux d'intérêt pour les arts américains.

"1995 onwards: the British composer Andrew Lloyd Webber
becomes the leader of a loyal group which reorganises financial
aid without an interest rate for American arts."

MUCH of this prediction would be incomprehensible were it not for other prophecies telling of seismic and economic disaster for America during this decade. The 'American arts' helped in this way could include not only stage productions, but films, as Hollywood is predicted to suffer a severe eclipse.

m o	q i	t b	s v	s n	t r	t g	e l	m d	s a	m d	e n	f o	q l	u r	e r
12	16	9	18	18	19	19	5	12	18	12	5	6	16	20	5
14	1:9	2	21	13	17	7	11	4	1	4	13	14	1	17	17
12	7	9	18	9	19	19	5	3	9	12	5	6	7	20	5
5	19	2	3	13	8	7	11	4	1·	4	4	5	1	8	8
Dec 197 May			27 Feb	Sep 16	198	197		May 16	24 Apr			Jun 95	7 Jan	2 0 0 8	May Aug

By 1995, intense efforts are in hand to revive American artistic productions, but raising finance will prove very difficult. The main stumbling block appears to be high rates of interest which could imperil the success of any projects and it seems likely that they fail.

However, by 16 April–24 May 1997, a group of concerned Europeans and Americans connected with business and the arts may come together to reorganise finance without an interest rate for a series of ventures.

During December 1997–May 1998, British interest may quicken. Andrew Lloyd Webber, composer of many famous musicals including *Cats*, *Phantom of the Opera* and *Aspects of Love*, could become interested or involved in the project. Between 16 February–27 September, he could be the leader of this loyal group of friends of American arts. It seems as if the group will be around for the next ten years, for it is not until May–August 2008 that American arts begin to flourish once again.

February 1993 X.89

Lloyd Webber fans outside Her Majesty's Theatre in London

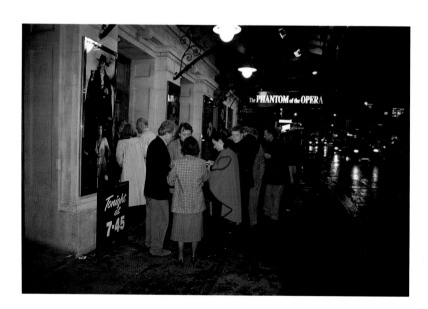

Stephen Hawking Explains the Universe

Cinq: Stephen Hawking jalonne une trainée radicale. Lace, cote
les dimensions de l'univers par subit, radieux tressage. Le
raccord paré sert matière en masse plié.

"From 1995, Stephen Hawking blazes a radical trail. He laces
up and classifies the dimensions of the universe by an unex-
pected, radiant weaving. The ornamental coupling sets matter
within the pleated mass, or whole."

STEPHEN Hawking is one of the most brilliant and admired theoretical physicists working today, despite being severely disabled by motor neurone disease.

Professor Hawking is most famous for his work on black holes, but according to this prediction his greatest achievements are yet to come.

Modern physics is seeking a unified theory of the universe – an explanation of how all known forces work together: gravity, electromagnetism and the weak and strong nuclear forces.

By the year 2000, the work of Stephen Hawking will have produced a series of original and daring proofs of such a theory. Nostradamus highlights its 'radical' and 'unexpected' qualities,

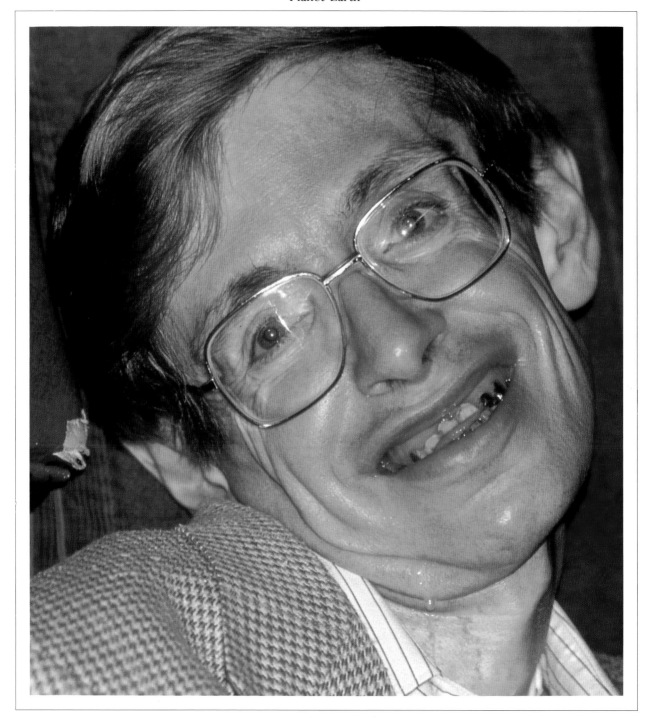

comparing it with the blaze of a comet across the dark night of previous scientific knowledge. The date 4 March 2000 is particularly significant, perhaps indicating the first presentation of the complete theory.

c	f	f	z	f	d	d	s	u	u	s	t	o	s
k	n	n	n	c	n	n	i	i	c	i	n	a	i
3	6	6	24	6	4	4	18	20	20	18	19	14	18
—	13	13	13	3	13	13	1:9	1:9	3	1:9	13	1	1:9
3	6	6	6	6	4	4	9	2	2	9	19	5	9
—	4	4	4	3	4	4	19	10	3	19	4	1	19
Mar	2	2	2		2000	4	199	2	Feb	199	194	5	199
	0	0	0	Mar	4	Apr						Jan	
	0	0	0						2003				
	0	0	0										

With beautiful simplicity it will answer our every question about the makeup of the physical universe — including why and how particles, the basic 'building blocks', react to forces and how these forces relate to one another.

As human beings, we are only aware of three spatial dimensions, plus a fourth — time. Physicists visualise as many as twenty-six, most of them curled up so small that for us they might as well not exist. Professor Hawking's work will not only reveal just how many dimensions there are, but will show connections between them in a revolutionary theory formulated by 4 April 1999.

To 'lace up' shoes, or the universe for that matter, you need two things — laces and holes to thread them through. In the universe the 'holes' might be black holes which are thought to occur when a star, having used up its fuel beyond a critical stage, collapses under the weight of its own mass. Under such stress a huge sun, or even part of a galaxy, can be reduced to a single point while retaining enormous gravitational 'pull' — literally a hole in the fabric of space.

Stephen Hawking, whose ideas have changed our perception of the universe

Some scientists have argued that a black hole may lead to other parts of the universe. Perhaps Nostradamus is saying that black holes act as connecting 'doorways' between the different dimensions.

According to Einstein, nothing can escape from a black hole, including light, the fastest known thing in the universe. 'Radiant weaving' may therefore refer to the parallel light rays which are always trying to escape from a black hole and never quite making it! This phrase may refer to brilliant developments within the study of light from 2 February 2003.

Work on black holes may hold the key to a new understanding of the universe. These strange phenomena may be gateways to other dimensions

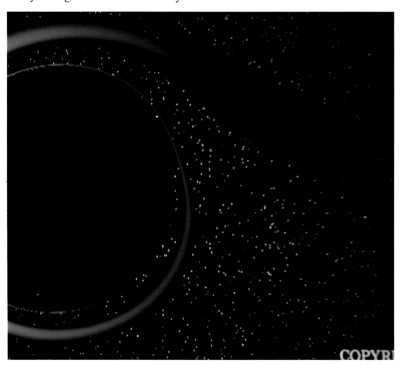

Between 1994–1999 the reasons for the existence of matter within the universe become known. Nostradamus talks of 'setting' matter like a jewel within the mass of the dimensions. Possibly matter is not an essential element of all the dimensions eventually discovered, but may only form when physical laws determine it. This idea may relate to the Big Bang theory, which proposes that the material universe within the dimensions that we know began at a particular point in time.

Astonishingly, Nostradamus states that the universe is 'pleated' – folded within itself perhaps an unimaginable number of times. The reality of this fact will be apparent by 5 January 1999.

Present-day physics argues that space is curved by the gravitational pull of each body within it, but this statement by Nostradamus goes much further and raises one of the great questions of modern physics – 'where is most of the universe?'

For the universe to act in the way that it does, we know that there must be about ninety per cent more matter than we can actually detect – called 'dark matter' by scientists.

The idea that the universe is 'pleated' or folded may be the key to this puzzle. In pleated material only the pleats themselves are visible. It is not until you stretch out the fabric that you can see how much material is 'hidden' by the pleats. If human beings have grown up seeing only the 'pleats' of the universe such a theory might set out to reveal its true dimensions, which Nostradamus is intent on comparing to a piece of jewellery in which the matched setting and precious stones make a thing of light and beauty.

There is overwhelming evidence in many of the predictions I have decoded that a revolution in scientific thinking, particularly in physics, is prophesied to occur from the middle of this decade and will continue throughout the first ten years of the new millennium. This new theory may be the key to that fundamental shift.

Inevitably, this interpretation must conclude that Nostradamus could himself have known the details of the new theory over four centuries ago.

The prediction is bursting with meaningful imagery, which I have tried to draw out, but in the end I believe that it is a special, private message sent across time for one man alone.

Stephen Hawking.

November 1991 11.51

Nuclear Fusion – A Blessing on Society

x   x   sp s   ʃ   p h sp   h

Cinq: la découverte de la fusion nucléaire par une sorte d'osmose

p u   h   s   s   t   p o

change vite la géographie industrielle d'Europe; or bénit la

u t u s   r t s

société à la manière nouvelle de vivre.

"1995 onwards: the discovery of nuclear fusion through a kind of osmosis swiftly alters the industrial geography of Europe; now it blesses society with a new way of living."

NUCLEAR fusion occurs when atoms of deuterium, present in immense quantities in sea water, collide to produce helium. This process, avoiding the side effects of enormous sun-like temperatures and gamma radiation, and predicted to be discovered in 1994, will transform the industrial geography of Europe within a few years. Energy provided by the fusion process will be inexpensive and almost limitless. Nuclear radioactivity produced by the current nuclear fission process will be a thing of the past.

This prediction describes the impact of the discovery, hailed during 21 November 1995–22 April 1996, as a brilliant European venture holding immense possibilities for society and industry alike. During 14 January–21 August 1995, trials continue, while during April–September interest spreads rapidly across the nations of Europe as the importance of the discovery is realised.

Between May 1996–January 1997, the benefits appear on the horizon, but it is not until 7 April 1998 that the industrial areas of Europe begin to be profoundly altered by the new process.

Inside the doughnut-shaped Torus reactor, based in Oxford, in which nuclear fusion experiments take place

| x | x | s | p | s | f | p | h | s | p | h | p | u | h | s | s | t | p | o | u | t | u | s | r | t | s |
l	v	e	l	i	a	a	n	e	d	e	g	t	g	d	d	e	i	a	c	a	l	a	l	d	v
22	22	19	15	18	6	15	8	18	15	8	15	20	8	18	18	19	15	14	20	19	20	18	17	19	18
11	21	5	11	1:9	1	1	13	5	4	5	7	19	7	4	4	5	1:9	1	3	1	11	1	11	4	21
22	4	19	6	9	6	15	8	9	15	8	6	20	8	9	9	19	6	5	20	10	20	9	8	19	9
11	21	5	11	19	1	1	13	5	4	5	7	10	7	4	4	5	19	1	3	1	11	1	2	4	21

22	Apr	Jun	199		21	Aug			23		Jun 2	98		Sep	196	May	2010	2009	2			199			
Nov	21	Nov			Jan 14		95	Apr 12		0	7 Apr	Apr		Jan	Mar 1	Nov1	0	Apr	21						
		195								1			195				0								
										0															

By 21 April 1999, it results in new industrial systems. New processes continue to emerge during November 1999–June 2000.

Between 2000–1 November 2009, nuclear fusion will gradually transform European society and by 12 April–23 June 2010, dramatic changes will have come about. 1 March is an important date in this process.

Computers Clash with Physics

```
       p          b   g        b   b              p
Après l'an deux mille, les ordinateurs font le traitement de
 p          e   f k  r                  p r r          r
l'information dans toute la terre. Fracassent un joug dur, un
    r        p    r        g
pratique fragile attaché à physique.
```

"After the year 2000, computers process information throughout
the world. They shatter a hard yoke, a fragile application of
theory linked with physics."

| p | b | g | b | b | p | p | e | f | k | r | p | r | r | r | r | p | r | g |
a	i	l	t	o	t	i	s	t	l	t	t	n	o	n	t	i	t	y
15	2	7	2	2	15	15	5	6	—	17	15	17	17	17	17	15	17	7
1	1:9	11	19	14	19	1:9	18	19	11	19	19	13	14	13	19	1:9	19	23
6	2	7	2	2	6	6	5	6	—	8	6	8	8	8	8	6	8	7
1	10	2	10	5	10	10	9	10	2	10	10	4	5	4	10	10	10	5
6	2	7	2	2	6	6	5	6		8	6	Aug 16			8	6	8	7
0		0		0	0		0			0					0	0	0	
0		0		0	0		0			0					0	0	0	
Jan	2	Feb	2	May	2	2	Sep	2	Feb	2	2	9 Apr			2	2	2	May

NOSTRADAMUS constantly returns in his predictions to the revolution in science, particularly physics, which will take place over the next two decades. To refer to it as an earthquake in scientific thinking would be an understatement.

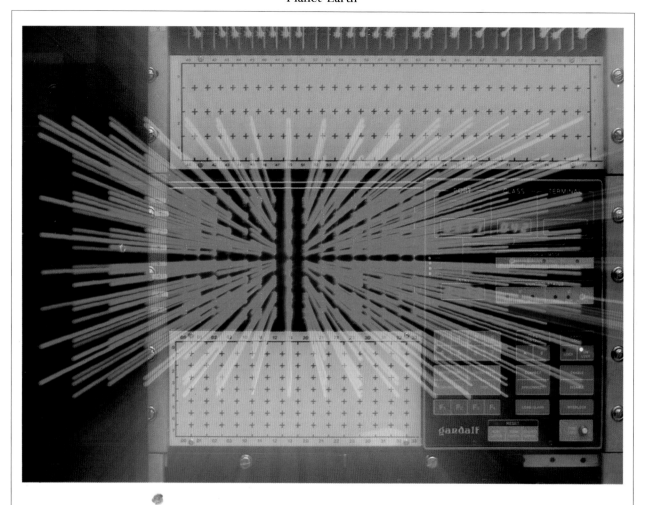

**Abstract photograph of
a close-up of the
Gandalf computer at the
CERN particle physics
laboratory, Geneva**

Here he describes the 'shattering' of a long-cherished theory — a 'hard yoke', as he puts it, since it has bound us for too long to a rigid view of the universe.

From 6 January 2002, computers of massive capacity will be stationed around the world and linked to one another by highly advanced exchanges of information systems. These computers, using millions of calculations per second, will form a pool of analysis for all kinds of scientific data, theories and results of experimentation.

Such a huge operation will take at least several years to get up and running, but dating suggests that the programme will begin producing data between 7 February 2002–2 May 2006.

By 2006, the weight of evidence gathered may have already begun to contradict what we at present believe to be one of the fundamental 'laws' of physics. Information strengthening this view will continue to emerge throughout that year.

Between 5 September 2006–February 2008, this new evidence will be discussed throughout the scientific world with many opposing its conclusions.

However, during 16 August 2008–9 April 2009, it is finally accepted that the evidence first visible in 2006 has clearly demonstrated the 'fragility' of a physics theory previously believed to be inviolable.

An important date in this process is 7 May 2008.

Although the prediction does not identify the physics theory which falls, it is possible that it is the Einsteinian principle that nothing in the universe can travel faster than light. Predictions of later decades indicate that the reality of super-light speeds is accepted by the scientific community — although the laws of physics familiar to us may not apply beyond the 'light barrier'.

October 1991 III.53

The Indispensable Robot

q   q   y h   q   u   e   r
Après l'an deux mille; en bref temps robots, larges et petits,
* u   c   y   e   m   e*
deviennent indispensables, un spectacle familier à la maison ou
*   i   i   q   u   e*
pendant qu'au travail. Fin cru fructueux.

"After the year 2000: in a short time robots, large and small,
become indispensable, a common sight at home or while at work.
A clever and profitable vineyard."

TO fill your time with leisure activities you would need to employ a group of people to carry out the day-to-day tasks you couldn't get around to doing for yourself. You would also need an independent income because you would be too busy to work. You would also have to pay for the services of those who provided these exciting activities. In other words, you would be rich.

But nowadays, even the rich worry themselves into the grave about their businesses, their country estates and their investments. What rich and poor alike need is someone to take over the dull, repetitive work that keeps home and business going, while leaving them to concentrate on the really important things in life – like organising society so that everyone can enjoy the dazzling range of goodies which technology is going to offer us in the next two decades.

Fortunately, such willing little helpers will soon be at hand!

In the year after 2000, robotics is set to introduce the concept of leisure in a bigger way than ever before to society. Those who think of robots as the clanking, metal entities from films in the fifties had better think again. Robotic technology is now developing a range of differently sized robots to do separate tasks. Many robots will resemble large insects, spiders and animals up to the size of a

q	q	y	h	q	u	e	r	u	c	y	e	m	e	i	i	q	u	e
a	l	l	n	p	b	l	p	v	p	l	l	l	a	a	a	v	n	x
16	16	23	8	16	20	5	17	20	3	23	5	12	5	1:9	1:9	16	20	5
1	11	11	13	15	2	11	15	21	15	11	11	11	1	1	1	21	13	22
7	7	5	8	7	20	5	8	20	3	5	5	12	5	10	10	7	20	5
1	2	2	4	15	2	11	15	3	6	2	11	11	1	1	1	3	4	22
		27	Jul	2		5 Aug		2				25 May		2	2	Jul	2005	
Jan	23			0		Nov15		0	Jun 25					0	0	Mar	Apr	22
				0				0						0	0			
				2				3						1	1			

dog – but many will look like no creature you ever heard of!

During 25 June 2001–25 May 2002, robots could begin to become a familiar sight around the home, cleaning the house, disposing of rubbish, checking callers, perhaps even carrying out basic tasks in the garden. *Calling all those saddled with mowing the lawn – your servitude is nearly at an end!*

During March–July 2001, robots may begin to infiltrate the workplace. Think of it – hundreds of thousands of workers who rarely break down, never phone in with a hangover disguised as a cold, don't need holidays or bonuses to keep working at the same pace, don't require pensions when they retire. Far from being thrown on the scrapheap, these workers can even be recycled!

At this point strong doubts may have entered your mind about how good this prospect really is. I know what you're thinking – if all these robots take over, what happens to jobs? How do people live if they can't earn money? The answer is that society will have to be reorganised. We will already have boundless, cheap supplies of energy and what robotics and other forms of technology will do is provide a whole new system of care for human beings. Technology could become so inexpensive, it might be dearer to employ an accounts department to invoice for it, than not to charge at all! It has been estimated that five per cent of the population, correctly organised, could make our clothes, build our houses, provide all our services and produce and distribute our food. The rest of us just need jobs so that we have the money to buy all these things.

However, suppose that that five per cent were robots – what would happen to the human population? They'd be sitting pretty, if you change the economics so that you pay the robots a minimum 'wage' to cover repair and replacement, and then cream off in enormous taxes the amount they and their companies earn. Financially, the rest of us would be their 'dependants', but would that truly matter if it left us free to learn, to design, to expand our horizons?

Barter, too, may play an important part. Using computer networks, people will be able to offer and seek services. For instance, if you're a lawyer and you want piano lessons for your daughter you could link up with a music teacher who wants legal advice. It won't matter if she lives hundreds of miles away – using fibre optics technology she will be able to teach your child without ever leaving home. (See 'Everyone A Space Voyager!')

This revolutionary social situation may emerge during the years 2002–5. Until 23 January 2002–27 July 2003, the select range of different robots limits the number of tasks carried out. But by 15 November 2003–5 August 2004, a change has happened. Diversification means that a new and skilful series of very large and very small robots may be able to perform complex tasks previously carried out by human beings.

By 22 April, robots have become a 'clever and profitable vineyard'. Robots have become intelligent. Their manufacture and distribution is a highly profitable exercise. Perhaps 'vineyard' suggests that they even enter the area of farming. Imagine a dairy where a spindly-looking robot moves silently from cow to cow linking them to milking equipment. The farmer is still sleeping. Out in the fields hundreds of other robots are also silently working.

But 'vineyard' also suggests one further possibility. Perhaps robots will have become so intelligent that they can make each other! Then the chain will be complete. The 'servants' won't need the 'master' at all and the 'master' will be free to leave and come back whenever he or she pleases.

A robot being tested in Boston Park, Mass. The cat watches a possible rival for human affections!

September 1992 X.89

Britain 2000 – Innovative Genius

x   *c*

Après l'an deux mille, le Royaume-Uni en l'Europe sera l'ogive

h   *p*   *h*   *s*   *o*

fusée d'esthétique et l'invention, or baches restent sur un

s   *p*   *o*   *u*   *s*

sophistiqué projet – copropriété avec France.

"After the year 2000, the United Kingdom in Europe will be the rocket nosecone of design and invention, but the covers remain over a sophisticated project – co-ownership with France."

WITHIN the political and economic freedoms of the new Europe after 2001, Britain's genius for design and invention flourishes during 2003–7.

By 11 July 2006, she may be heavily involved in new forms of innovative rocket design, but she will have many other inventions to her credit since 2000.

x	c	h	p	h	s	o	s	p	o	u	s
y	e	e	i	l	a	n	q	j	i	e	e
22	3	8	15	8	18	14	18	15	14	20	18
23	5	5	1:9	11	1	13	16	10	1:9	5	5
4	3	8	6	8	9	5	9	6	5	2	9
5	5	5	10	2	1	4	7	10	10	5	5
July 11		8	2	2	2	May 9		6	5		
2000		May 0	0	0				0	0	2	Sep
			0	0	0			0	0		
			2	0	0	4	Jul	2	2	May 5	

Concorde. State of the Art technology produced by Britain and France and destined to pale into insignificance beside the secret Anglo-French project for after the year 2000

From 4 July 2000–9 May 2001, she will be initiating a sophisticated new project, not completed or revealed until 2006.

During 2 September 2005–5 May 2006, this project will need extra scientific development and finance which will come from France in return for an equal share in prestige and rewards.

Even though he may know the details of the project, Nostradamus does no more than hint at them. It will be kept secret, probably for commercial reasons, for several years. For Nostradamus to have described it in advance would mean that this part of the prediction would fail.

Possibly connected with space technology, it would have to be a major project. Previous collaborations between the two countries have produced Concorde, the world's only supersonic commercial airliner, and the Channel Tunnel linking England and France beneath the sea.

October 1991 VII.14

Europe 2000 – Scientific Superpower

        b   *b*   *m*
Après l'an deux mille, continent nu de l'Europe, quitte de
u   *i*   *q*   *m* *q u*
contraintes passées, tête de la terre sic, renoue fruits de science.
u *f*   *m*   *m* *q* *u*
La physique y fait rafraîchir sans nuages.

"After the year 2000, the undisguised continent of Europe, free of past restraints, the head of the world — this is so — renews the fruits of science. Here physics refreshes in an unclouded future."

Stacked 'Chunnel' linings at Calais. Europe, including Britain, will be a superstate whose power is based on dazzling technology

NOSTRADAMUS emphasises Europe's dominance early in the next millennium, using the Latin *sic* – this is so – to drive this point home. She replaces America in this role.

By 2002–5 Europe will have become a political and economic federation, possibly extending from Ireland to the borders of China. Old divisions stifling European creativity are no more, the

b	b	m	u	i	q	m	q	u	u	f	m	m	q	u
e	l	e	c	s	l	e	d	s	l	h	t	r	n	a
2	2	12	20	1:9	16	12	16	20	20	6	12	12	16	20
5	11	5	3	18	11	5	4	18	11	8	19	17	13	1
2	2	3	20	10	7	3	7	20	20	6	3	3	7	20
5	2	5	3	9	2	5	4	9	2	8	10	8	4	1
2	2	Mar	2	2	July	3	July	2	2	Jun	3	3	Jul	2
0	0		0	0				0	0	Aug	0			0
0	0	May	0	0	Feb	May	4	0	0		0	Aug	4	0
5	2		3	9				9	2		2			1

last having disappeared by May 2003–March 2004. After February–July 2009, Europe leads the world (see 'European Parliament – World Government').

Through revolutionary new scientific discoveries, the 'fruits of science' – new technologies – will be flourishing by 4 May–2 July 2009.

During August 2002–June 2003, our understanding of the physical universe will make enormous strides and many previously intractable problems will be solved. These developments may be connected with predictions (See section on TRAVEL IN SPACE) in which Nostradamus predicts that human beings will have travelled almost to the outer limits of the solar system by 2009.

4 August 2001–3 July 2002 will give an early signal of this quantum leap in knowledge.

Note: I have substituted the single letter f for ph in *physique*. By itself the combination produces the date 2000, suggesting a major scientific advance in that year, possibly new thinking in physics (See 'Stephen Hawking Explains the Universe').

    f   6   6
ph15 8 6 8 = 20 = 2000

October 1991 X.89

H E A L T H

... and the frontiers of medicine advance while plague still continues to threaten ...

A Cure for AIDS

---

b		b		b		h		h		f				r

Cinq: un vaccin de la maladie AIDS est developpé en l'Europe.

k		r		r				p		r		r		r

En l'Allemagne les patient déjà mal font une reprise après

		r		p				r		f				

guérir à genetique. Fort rugueux fuira.

"From 1995 a vaccine for the disease AIDS is developed in Europe. in Germany patients already ill recover after cure by genetics. A rugged fortress takes flight."

THIS prediction holds out hope of a cure for the terrible disease AIDS, projected to infect tens of millions throughout the world by the year 2000.

Dating begins within *cinq*/1995, when a vaccine against AIDS could be developed in Europe. Several countries may take part. Significant dates are 2 March, 2 May and 8 May. By August, the vaccine is ready to use, perhaps first among those sections of the community most at risk.

The vaccine will only be effective in *preventing* infection. Those who have full-blown AIDS will not be helped.

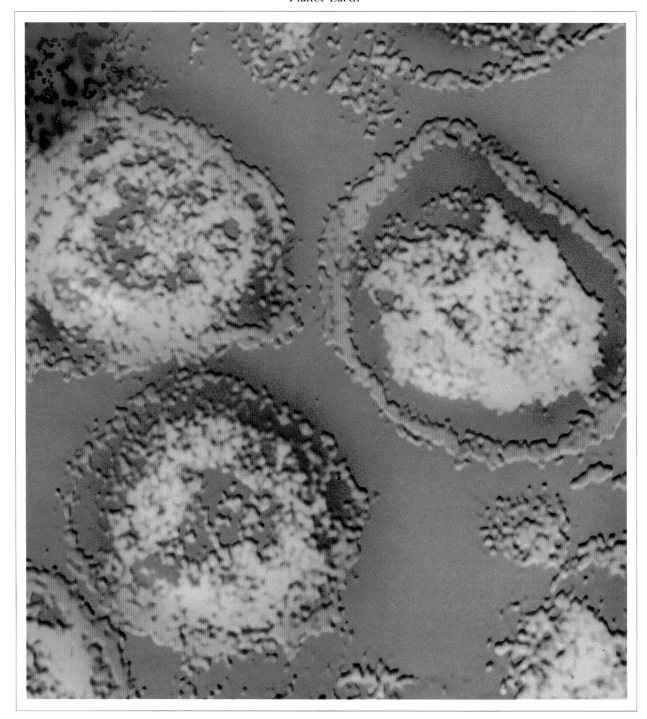

b	b	b	h	h	f	r	k	r	r	p	r	r	r	r	p	r	f
c	v	e	e	e	v	n	n	l	l	l	n	i	e	i	i	e	i
2	2	2	8	8	6	17	–	17	17	15	17	17	17	17	15	17	6
3	21	5	5	5	21	5	13	11	11	11	13	1:9	5	1:9	1:9	5	1:9
2	2	2	8	8	6	8	–	8	8	6	8	8	8	8	6	8	6
3	3	5	5	5	3	5	4	2	2	2	4	19	5	19	19	5	19
2	2	2	8	8		Aug											
Mar	Mar	May	May	May	9	5	44					198	8	198	196	8	196
													May			May	

Nevertheless, there may be a German breakthrough in 1996, involving alteration of the virus by genetics, making it harmless. Those who have AIDS will, it seems, be cured.

Complete success could be announced by 8 May 1998, after a two-year period of observation. Experimentation will begin with the first group of patients on 8 May 1996. The central dating section beginning with k totals 44, perhaps the initial number of volunteers.

After decoding I seldom refer back to the original quatrain, but in this case Prophecy III.53 – from which this prediction is drawn – names 'Nuremberg', 'Ausburg', 'Basle' and 'Frankfurt', places which may be connected with this research.

**Opposite page: colour scanning of the HIV virus, an illness which is destined to be defeated in the next few years.
Left: a virus penetrating and infecting a white blood cell**

November 1991 III.53

Plague in India

<pre>
  h   p   r   o   u   v
Mort – un quart de l'Inde parce que les cités populeux
          o   i   o   o   s g
contractent une maladie rare. Une grosse fièvre sanglante dure
s   s   y   p   h
jusqu'à malades perdent ses sens.
</pre>

"*Dead – a quarter of India, because the crowded cities contract a rare disease. A high bloody fever lasts until the patients become unconscious.*"

INDIA has a population of over 700 million, so the effects of 1 in 4 dying during 1996–8 cannot be imagined. Although the prediction appears to state this, it may instead be saying that this mortality rate occurs only in a certain quarter or area of the country.

An abandoned corpse in Calcutta. The plague Nostradamus predicts may enter India from another country

h	p	r	o	u	v	o	i	o	n	o	s	g	s	s	y	p	h
t	t	c	q	t	x	t	e	l	a	s	t	d	j	l	d	e	s
8	15	17	14	20	21	14	1:9	14	13	14	18	7	18	18	23	15	8
19	19	3	16	19	22	19	5	11	1	18	19	4	10	11	4	5	18
8	6	8	5	2	3	5	19	5	4	5	9	7	9	9	5	6	8
19	19	3	7	19	4	19	5	2	1	9	19	4	1	2	4	5	9
198-196		Aug 10			195		May	Apr 95	199		Jul		99		May 6	98	
		29	Apr		195	Feb	Jan			Apr	Jan	2	4 May				

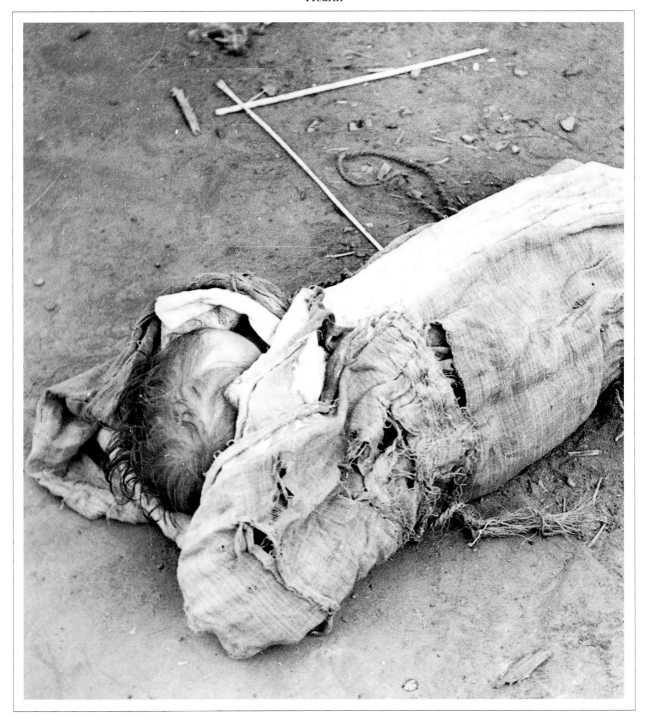

Nostradamus, himself a doctor, is precise – the disease arises in India's crowded cities between 10 August 1995–29 April 1996. At that point, it is a rare condition, but a genetic mutation may occur to enable it to spread rapidly after April 1995–January 1996.

Inevitably, between 6 May 1998–4 May 1999, the country is unable to cope with the scale of the tragedy and after 2 January 1999, no form of care may be offered to the sick. During July 1999–April 2000, the disease shows no sign of slackening.

Its most obvious symptom is a 'high bloody fever' which lasts until unconsciousness sets in. 'Blood' could refer to blood being emitted from the patient's mouth and other orifices of the body, or it could mean the collapse of blood vessels, gradually reddening the skin.

December 1990 III.65

Lasers Treat Heart Disease

---

v   g   b   p   q   b b
Cinq: le traitement de la maladie de coeur comprend chirurgie
f   r   r   t   r   t   b
de technologie laser sous anesthésie locale. La braque sur les
r   q   m   r   t   q u
tubes usés. Ne fait pas subir un coup de couteaux.

*"1995 onwards: the treatment of heart disease includes surgery
using laser technology under local anaesthetic. It aims at worn-
out tubes. Cutting with knives no longer prevails."*

DURING 8 March–19 August 1995, laser surgery may be used with a local anaesthetic to treat a variety of conditions.

Between 9 March–16 May 1996, the possibility opens up of being able to extend this treatment.

v	g	b	p	q	b	b	f	r	r	t	r	t	b	r	q	m	r	t	q	u
c	n	e	i	c	n	c	d	h	s	o	h	c	e	s	n	i	i	n	d	c
21	7	2	15	16	2	2	6	17	17	19	17	19	2	17	16	12	17	19	16	20
3	13	5	1:9	3	13	3	4	8	18	14	8	3	5	18	13	1:9	1:9	13	4	3
3	7	2	6	7	2	2	6	17	8	19	8	19	2	8	7	12	8	19	7	20
3	13	5	19	3	13	3	4	8	9	5	8	3	5	9	4	10	10	4	4	3
Mar	9		196	Jul	27				98		Aug 19		Feb 98		19 Aug			197		2
	16	May			23			Aug	195	8 Mar		May			2004			Apr 4		0
																				0
																				3

Laser surgery–it could replace the scalpel altogether

From 4 April 1997, lasers could treat blocked arteries and veins of the heart. During February–May 1998, this treatment may prove so successful that, during 27 July – 23 August 1998, major heart operations may take place using this technique.

Throughout 2003 to 19 August 2004, the use of manual surgery, using instruments such as scalpels, may be considerably reduced, hinting at laser surgery being extended to many kinds of minor and major operations.

March 1993 I.28

Schizophrenia – A Food Allergy?

f   f g   a
Cinq: le traitement de la schizophrénie comprend l'entendement
d a a a   d l
juste du cerveau comme récepteur sensible aux grosses facteurs en
s i s
la nourriture. Les sasse.

"1995 onwards: the treatment of schizophrenia includes the accurate understanding of the brain as a receiver sensitive to key factors in food. It sifts them."

| f | f | g | a | d | a | a | d | a | d | l | s | i | s |
m	r	n	n	t	e	m	c	n	c	n	n	e	e
6	6	7	1	4	1	1	4	1	4	11	18	1:9	18
12	17	13	13	19	5	12	3	13	3	13	13	5	5
6	6	7	1	4	1	1	4	1	4	2	9	19	9
12	8	4	4	10	5	3	3	4	3	4	4	5	5
Jun	14			4						13	Sep		
		24	Apr	0	May	21					195	95	
				0									
				2									

RESEARCH into functions of the brain throughout 1995, especially during 21 May–13 September, reveals just how sensitive this biological computer is to key factors in food. Normally, the brain will sift or screen out any factors which threaten dysfunction, but in a certain proportion of the population the brain may be genetically allergic to these factors, or

**A dried-food shop in
Hong Kong**

could have become sensitised to chemicals in food, or pollutants in the environment. Symptoms of schizophrenia include aural and visual hallucination and it must be remembered that certain naturally occurring elements in food are hallucinogenic. Perhaps some human brains are abnormally allergic to these substances.

Over the years research produces an increasingly accurate understanding of the way the brain works so that, by 14 June 2004 – 24 April 2005, the treatment of schizophrenia could become much more effective.

February 1993 II.51

Compulsory Sport for Over-Forties

a   a   a   f   a c f b   a   a
Cinq: le sport devient l'expérience de toute une vie aux centres
l f   o   r   c   a c   o
gratuits où on y force l'homme, la femme plus de
a   i   r   a
quadragénaire à garder le corps.

"1995 onwards: sport becomes a lifetime's experience in free cen-
tres where each man and woman over forty is compelled to look
after the body."

'FEELING good' through fitness became one of the great icons of the eighties. Sport was no longer practised by an élite group. Millions of people discovered what it was like to run long distances, including the marathon. Health farms, workouts and body-building became part of social culture.

The accent on fitness is set to continue with special emphasis on the over-forties to prevent the onset of conditions like heart disease and brittle bones.

With dazzling technologies on offer in the home, the next decade could produce even more 'couch-potatoes' – people slumped in front of the television who never take any exercise. To counterbalance this influence, fitness will have to become a necessary part of the social equation – essential to the prolonged health and vigour of older people. For this age group there could be an element of compulsion in taking exercise – if not legal, at least educational and social.

a	a	a	f	a	c	f	b	a	a	l	f	o	r	c	a	c	o	a	i	r	a
e	t	v	x	e	t	u	v	x	t	t	u	y	e	m	m	u	e	u	g	e	p
1	1	1	6	1	3	6	2	1	1	11	6	14	17	3	1	3	14	1	1:9	17	1
5	19	21	22	5	19	20	21	22	19	19	20	23	5	12	12	20	5	20	7	5	15
1	1	1	6	1	3	6	2	1	1	11	6	5	17	3	1	3	14	1	19	8	1
5	10	21	4	5	10	20	21	4	10	10	20	23	5	3	12	20	5	20	7	5	6
Jan	1	Jan	10		6	Feb	1	1	Nov	6	May	21			3	May	1			Aug	1
May	0		30	Oct	0	21	Apr	0	Oct	0			31	Dec	0			0	197	5	Jun
	0				0			0							0			0			
	2				2			2							2			2			

Between 5 June–August 1997, there emerges a new emphasis on looking after the body, including preventative medicine and checkups, diet and exercise. This development may result from increased knowledge of what makes the body work and how we become ill.

By January–May 2001, many over-forties could be encouraged to spend more time at sports centres offering incentives to join (a hint that retirement age may also be lowered).

During 21 May–31 December 2003, regular exercise may become compulsory.

Between 10–30 October 2006, sport will have become a necessary part of everyone's life, an essential ingredient for a balanced, healthy community. To make access even easier, sessions and entrance to sports centres are free. Considerable government subsidy could be involved.

An elderly keep-fit class in Sun City, Arizona

The Old Become Young

---

b   b   b   b   h   b
Cinq: le rajeunissement comprend la manipulation génétique que
b   t u b   r   r
produit sur le tard un visage sans rides, un corps fort et ferme.
t   l   p   q   u
Alors, quelle égalité d'or est rendue aux agés!

"1995 onwards: rejuvenation includes genetic manipulation
which produces late in life a face without wrinkles and a strong,
firm body. What golden equality is then restored to the elderly!"

Will creams and preparations promising to restore youth become redundant by 2007?

RESEARCH into genetic techniques of rejuvenation produces the first real signs of success in 2000, probably in trials with a group of volunteers. During April–August, treatments could restore vigour to their bodies. The psychological impact cannot be overestimated. Older people feel greatly disadvantaged as their bodies grow weaker and less able to respond instantly to the brain's commands. A joyful sense of equality will accompany the return of youth.

This growing success is followed during August 2001–April 2002 by the banishment of facial lines and wrinkles. Between 2 February–13 May 2002 rejuvenation has become a major issue, with ever rising demand for this treatment.

I detect that, up until this point, research will have been concentrated on patients of fifty years old, or less. However, during April–August 2004, trials may begin with an older group in their sixties, seventies and eighties. This research will continue between 14 April 2004–19 February 2005, with a special concentration on the face from October 2004.

The research peaks during 21 April–26 July 2007, when the elderly begin to be restored to golden youth.

b	b	b	b	h	b	b	t	u	b	r	a	r	t	l	p	q	u
n	e	j	n	n	n	o	d	n	i	n	i	n	i	d	s	n	g
2	2	2	2	8	2	2	19	20	2	17	1	17	19	11	15	16	20
13	5	10	13	13	13	14	4	13	1:9	13	1:9	13	1:9	4	18	13	7
2	2	2	2	8	2	2	19	20	2	8	1	8	10	11	15	7	20
13	5	10	4	4	4	14	4	4	10	4	10	4	10	4	8	13	7
Feb	2	2	2	Aug	2	Feb	19	2	Feb	Aug	1	Aug	2	26		Jul	2
13	May	0	0	Apr	0	14	Apr	0	Oct	Apr	0	Apr	0	Apr 21			0
		0	0		0			0			0		0				0
		2	4		4			4			2		0				7

If this prediction proves to be true, then current speculation on how to cope with an ageing population is irrelevant. Instead, we would face a different but no less formidable set of problems. How, for instance, do you tell sixty-year-old men and women with the health and vigour of thirty-year-olds that they are too 'old' to work?

Such a development would have huge social consequences for jobs, welfare, housing and birth control. Other predictions in this book suggest some answers to these tricky questions. Discrimination on the grounds of age would become superfluous.

October 1992 I.28

TRANSPORT

*... and people are free to walk the cities once
more, while the car becomes a computer ...*

The Channel Tunnel

      r   *g*   *i*

Le Tunnel de la Manche joint la France et Angleterre. Sans

      v   *p*   *i o*

aucun doute prouvera que sans réseau des chemins sera trop de

  n   *g*   *y*   *p*

poids pour les rues tous deux.

*"The Channel Tunnel joins France and England. Undoubtedly, it
will prove that, without a network of roads, there will be too
much weight for the streets in both."*

I N 1990, French and English workers first met through the wall
of a spur tunnel linking the two main tunnels being built from
England and France. The tunnel is due to be opened in 1993.
However, by 19 January 1995, it will have become obvious
that at least one side has not made adequate road provision to
carry the weight of traffic away from the Tunnel. Much of the
freight will have to pass over streets which were never constructed to bear such stress (7 April 1995–4 February 1996).
Roads could begin to give way, damaging supply systems such as
water, electricity, sewage, gas and telecommunications.

Eurotunnel – in the entrance on the English side of the Channel

| r | g | i | v | p | i | o | n | g | y | p |
d	e	t	t	c	a	t	d	l	t	x
17	7	1:9	21	15	1:9	14	13	7	23	15
4	5	19	19	3	1	19	4	11	19	22
8	7	10	3	6	19	5	4	7	5	6
4	5	10	10	3	1	19	4	2	19	4
8	Jul	2	3	Jun	195		Apr 7	195		2
Apr 5		0	0	Mar	Jan 19	4	Feb			0
		0	0							0
		0	2							0

By the year 2000, this problem will have also developed at the other exit from the Tunnel. During 5 April–8 July, France and England may have to join forces to defeat the problem.

The final period June 2003–March 2004 indicates that crumbling road surfaces may force a completely new attitude in creating an effective network of roads leading away from each exit. Alternatively, this may not be necessary (see 'AntiGravity Flying Machines').

Note: the Tunnel is scheduled to open in 1994 with Queen Elizabeth and President Mitterrand making an inaugural journey together on 6 May.

January 1992 III.65

**A Texaco petrol station
in New York in the
1930s**

Road Transport Revolutionised

   x   *d*   *q*   *e*   *d*

Les gens voyagent par les transports en commun sans payer.

   b   *l* *q*   *e*   *c*   *c*   *e*   *d*

L'automobile cède au loi, fuira limites des cités. Au chemin

   d *i*   *i*

l'ordinateur est le chauffeur.

"People travel by public transport without paying. The car sur-renders to the law, it will avoid city limits. On the road, the computer is the driver."

TRANSPORT has become one of the biggest civil problems. This prediction describes some solutions which will
begin to be implemented towards the end of this decade.
1998 will focus on the human driver versus the electronic
'brain' which will eventually take over the driver's function com-

| x | d | q | e | d | b | l | q | e | c | c | e | d | d | i | i |
y	r	p	o	y	o	u	o	f	m	s	u	m	r	s	r
22	4	16	5	4	2	11	16	5	3	3	5	4	4	1:9	1:9
23	17	15	14	23	14	20	14	6	12	18	20	12	17	18	17
4	4	7	5	4	2	2	7	5	3	3	5	4	4	19	19
5	8	6	5	5	5	2	5	6	3	9	2	3	8	9	8
	8	Jul	2	Apr	22						5	4	Apr		
May	14		0						26	Sep	0	Mar	8	199	198
			0								0				
			0								2				

pletely. Human drivers take chances, drive when ill or drunk, fall asleep, misjudge distances and carry out bad manoeuvres. The electronic 'driver' installed in many cars won't do any of these things. Cars driven by computer may become frequent during 8 March–4 April 1999.

By 14 May–8 July 2000, great resources will be directed by many countries into providing cheap public transport for the people, so saving on road maintenance, traffic congestion and environmental pollution.

Between 22 April–26 September 2005, public transport in most areas will be free of charge and centrally funded by governments. Cars will be subject to strict laws, one of which will ban it from all major cities.

January 1991 I.42

Anti-Gravity Flying Machines

---

      u   *p*   *b* *q*   *q*   *b*

Après l'an deux mille, on devient possible d'éviter la loi de la

      b   *u*   *ƒg*   *u*   *u*   *t*

pesanteur à la terre. On se met à construire des machines au but

     b   *r*   *q*   *u*   *r*   *t*   *l*   *q*   *u*

de transporter chaque fois un grand nombre de gens.

"After the year 2000: it becomes possible to bypass the law of gravity on Earth. Machines begin to be constructed for the purpose of transporting a great number of people at one time."

THE theory and technology described are at present unknown. The prediction fastens on the fact that anti-gravity machines. able to transport 'a great number of people at one time', will be constructed in the next century.

u	p	b	q	q	b	b	u	f	g	u	u	t	b	r	q	u	r	t	l	q	u
d	n	n	o	v	a	n	e	n	s	n	d	i	d	n	h	i	n	n	o	d	n
20	15	2	16	16	2	2	20	6	7	20	20	19	2	17	16	20	17	19	11	16	20
4	13	13	14	21	1	13	5	13	18	13	4	1:9	4	13	8	1:9	13	13	14	4	13
20	6	2	16	16	2	2	2	6	7	20	20	10	2	8	16	20	8	19	11	7	20
4	13	13	5	3	1	13	5	4	18	4	4	19	4	4	8	10	13	4	5	4	4
2	Jun 18		18 Feb			2	6 Jul		2	2		Oct 26			2	Aug 19			11	Jul	2
0		26 May	Mar 14			0	Apr 18		0	0				27 Aug		13 Apr				May 4	0
0						0	0		0	0						1					0
4						5	4		4	4						0					4

**At the beginning of this century men still dreamed of flight,
impossible though it seemed. Now the technology is set to undergo
a second revolution as aircraft conquer the forces of gravity itself**

Today, major airports are stretched to capacity for one reason
– gravity. This force limits the size of aircraft and the weight
they carry, because aeroplanes must possess enough engine power
to fight gravity before getting into the air. To meet ever-growing
demand, thousands of aircraft have to take off and land every
day. The only answer is to build more airports, but, like the

building of more roads, planned airports immediately arouse public resistance in the areas for which they are targeted.

With anti-gravity machines, these restrictions would be swept aside. Ten or twenty thousand people could be transported at a time, because if you could 'switch off' gravity, or lessen gravitational pull to enable the machine to 'float', capacity would no longer be limited by the amount of power needed to get off the ground. A small motor would drive the aircraft in the required direction. The economics of air travel would be transformed overnight. So would the aircraft industry which would have to adapt rapidly to avoid becoming obsolete.

Possibilities include continent-to-continent journeys, cross-country 'hops' (each town could have its own airport, like a bus or coach station), and monorail systems for large cities.

One or more of these machines begin to be constructed during 18 April–6 July 2004 – a watershed year for this technology, with people being experimentally transported during 4 May – 11 July, while the social possibilities in such a mode of travel could dawn on the media during 26 May–18 June.

Between 27 August–26 October, more machines could be constructed.

During 14 March 2005–18 February 2006, the dream opens up of being able to bypass the law of gravity in many ways that profoundly affect the organisation of society.

By 13 April–19 August 2010, these innovations will have produced great changes. Possibilities include beautiful, fragile-looking cities floating permanently in the air and private land-and-sea skimmers, enabling people to travel anywhere and everywhere. International frontiers could become meaningless.

E C O L O G Y

... while the mother planet is poisoned ...

Pollution Damages the World

>   *y*   *x*   *y*   *x*   *u*
> *Je vois la pollution chimique gagnant sur les champs du monde*
>   *y*   *e*   *x*   *y*   *u*   *u*
> *et la mer puante, arrivé à son nadir. Surir le bel air des monts.*
>   *r*   *e*
> *Le cru lève une cueillette cruelle.*

> "I see chemical pollution creeping over the fields of the world
> and the stinking sea reaching its lowest point. The beautiful air
> of the mountains will turn sour. The vineyard raises a cruel har-
> vest."

| y | x | y | x | u | y | e | x | y | u | u | r | e |
o	t	n	h	m	t	t	a	a	a	t	n	t
23	22	23	22	20	23	5	22	23	20	20	17	5
14	19	13	8	13	19	19	1	1	1	19	13	19
5	4	5	4	2	5	5	4	5	20	20	8	5
5	19	4	8	4	19	19	1	1	1	10	4	19
		95	Apr	2	195	195	Apr	May	2	2	8	195
May	23		8	Apr			Jan	1	0	0	Apr	
									0	1		
									1	0		

The ravaging effect of pollution: *left* **a rubbish tip in Mexico City** *right* **the heavily industrialised Cheripoviets in Russia**

MANY people would argue that we have reached the state of pollution described, but Nostradamus indicates we have still some way to go. By introducing a personal note – 'I see' – he emphasises the strength of this particular vision and its warning.

This prediction focuses strongly on the year 1995 when chemical residues are found to be poisoning fields throughout the world, affecting crops and domesticated animals. During 2 April–23 May a stream of reports may focus on the poisoning of land and sea alike (see 'Talking to Dolphins – A Breakthrough'). 8 April may signal a harvest of crops too poisoned to eat.

By January 1996, seas and oceans may be so badly affected that they stink of chemicals and waste products poured into them every day.

The entire situation described here will be at its worst from 1 May 2001. Eventually, even the once pure air of the mountains will leave a bad taste in the mouth (2010).

Nostradamus uses 'vineyard' in its Biblical sense of humanity's responsibility for the management of the earth. The 'harvest' produced by mismanagement of the vineyard rebounds on millions of people.

January 1991 I.35

South America – Laws to Protect Resources

l   d   x   u   l   h
Cinq: Amerique du Sud couchante – Brésil, Mexique, entre pays
a   a   o   d
autres, dodelinent des têtes à homologuer géographie campée
l   a   m   a   o
avant produire code de cambrousse.

"1995 onwards: South America to the west – Brazil and
Mexico, among other countries, nod heads to the ratification of
a fixed geography, before producing a statutory code of the
countryside."

l	d	x	u	l	h	a	a	o	d	l	a	m	a	o
q	q	e	s	q	y	e	e	i	e	t	i	e	e	b
11	4	22	20	11	8	1	1	14	4	11	1	12	1	14
16	16	5	18	16	23	5	5	1:9	5	19	1:9	5	5	2
2	4	4	2	2	8	1	1	5	4	11	1	3	1	5
7	7	5	9	7	5	5	5	19	5	10	10	5	5	2
		10	Feb		98	Jan	1	May	4	Nov	1	Mar	6	
Jul	7	95			May		2000	195	2000		2000		2000	Feb

South America: the Amazonian rain forest

THE prediction focuses on western South America, indicating that action may be forced upon the countries concerned, partly because of geological changes caused by earthquakes and resulting climatic shift. At stake may be the future of the South American rain forests as crucial to the correction of the ecological balance.

During 1995, Brazil may be the first country to recognise the need for a survey of geographical features and the realignment of internationally agreed borders. A proposal for a detailed survey lasting several years may be proposed on 4 May. During 7 July 1995 – 10 February 1996, Brazil, recognising her ecological responsibilities, may attempt to interest her neighbours in a joint survey.

However, it may not be until May 1998 that Mexico and other countries will join in such a venture.

1 January 2000 marks a preliminary agreement between these countries to develop an international statutory code governing the preservation of ecological resources. The code could be formulated during February–6 March. Ratification may take place on 1 November.

Australasia – The Greenhouse Effect

j   s   f   s   f   g
Cinq: temps fugace, brulant – la détérioration de l'économie
    s   x   r   r s   m   s
de l'Australie hate une tirade, pendant que la Nouvelle-Zélande
s   s   s c   s
deviendra plus d'une serre chaude.

"A short, burning time – the deterioration of the Australian economy hastens a tirade, while New Zealand will become more of a hothouse."

THE greenhouse effect caused by the build-up of carbon dioxide and other gases in the atmosphere will, Nostradamus predicts, profoundly alter the weather systems of both Australia and New Zealand over the next decade.

j	s	f	s	f	g	s	x	r	r	s	m	s	s	s	s	c	s
n	e	a	a	n	l	u	n	d	n	q	n	l	v	l	d	n	d
10	18	6	18	6	7	18	22	17	17	18	12	18	18	18	18	3	18
13	5	1	1	13	11	20	13	4	13	16	13	11	21	11	4	13	4
10	9	6	9	6	7	9	4	8	8	9	3	9	9	9	9	3	9
4	5	1	1	4	2	2	4	4	4	7	4	2	3	2	4	4	4
Oct	96			97			12 Aug			Mar		99			99	3 Sep	
Apr 95		1	Jan		2 Feb		Apr 8		97		Apr 5		Feb 12				

Australia is the first to be affected from April–October 1995, reaching a peak around 1 January 1996, the height of the Australian summer. This 'short, burning time' may produce excessively high temperatures, together with widespread out-breaks of bush fires and the destruction of grazing lands for cattle and sheep. The change in weather patterns will continue so that, by 2 February 1997, it will be damaging the Australian economy. Angry public debate will follow as people begin to realise the economic implications of what is happening (8 April–12 August). 2000 marks a low point in the economy.

New Zealand has a longer time in which to prepare for a somewhat different future.

Change will gradually alter the climate until 6 March 1999, when it will become evident that the temperate weather she used to enjoy has disappeared. Since New Zealand becomes 'more of a hothouse' it can be assumed that this means she will experience higher temperatures and a greatly increased humidity (3 September 1999–12 February 2000). Her agricultural industry is vital to New Zealand and this prediction may be taken as a warning to her to 'switch' some of her agriculture to the production of fruits, veg-etables and crops which can easily be grown in such conditions.

By the end of the year 2000 the alteration to a 'jungle' climate will have become too great to be unmistakable.

April 1992 II.51

Chemistry Halts Industrial Pollution

y   p   p   u o f
Cinq: l'industrie frustrée, jusqu'en dégagée de pollution.

r   s   r   s   s   s
Développements brevetés à la chimie mènent à une

s   r   n u   r   r
transformation superbe en la culture freinée de consommation.

"1995 onwards: industry frustrated, until set free of pollution. Patented developments in chemistry lead to a superb transformation in a slowed-down consumer culture."

An oxygen bar in a Tokyo department store. Customers inhale oxygen to counter the effects of city pollution

y	p	p	u	o	f	r	s	r	s	s	s	s	r	n	u	r	r
t	e	e	g	d	l	m	e	a	i	m	e	m	e	a	l	i	a
23	15	15	20	14	6	17	18	17	18	18	18	18	17	13	20	17	17
19	5	5	7	4	11	12	5	1	1:9	12	5	12	5	1	11	1:9	1
5	15	6	20	5	6	8	9	8	9	9	9	9	8	4	20	8	8
19	5	5	7	4	11	12	5	10	19	12	5	12	5	1	2	19	10
195	15	Jun	2	May	6	Aug		Aug	199	Sep			98	198	Apr	2	Aug
May	5		0	4	Nov	Dec	95	Oct		Dec	95	Dec	5		Jan	0	Oct
			0													0	
			7													2	

THE prediction opens with a reference to 'frustrated industry', indicating that many new laws and regulations preventing pollution may now be seriously hindering industrial production (15 June 1995–5 May 1996).

However, during December 1995–August 1996, new discoveries in chemical research will be patented. By September, they are leading to a 'superb transformation' (5 December 1995) in consumer culture which has reached a very low ebb during August–October. This does suggest that because pollution arising from industrial processes can now be avoided, existing companies will be free to expand and many new companies can be set up, using this new process from the beginning. Unemployment may begin to fall.

Between August–October 1999 and January–April 2002 these chemical developments are having a dramatic effect on a society now regarding ecological needs as one of its main priorities.

During 4 November 2007–6 May 2008, pollution may no longer be a factor in many areas of production (sadly, this does not necessarily mean that the problems of pollution caused in previous years have gone away).

March 1993 IX.36

R E L I G I O N

... and the West turns to old beliefs ...

Cardinal Hume Elected Pope

>   *c*   *p*   *n*   *s n*
> *Quand Karol — fer voué — meurt, Cardinal George Basil Hume*
>   *s*   *s u*   *u*   *n*   *s*   *j*
> *sera élu Pontife en Angleterre d'où voyage nu avec prière au sud*
> *s e*   *o* *p*   *h*
> *d'Europe peu sure, sans signer.*

> "When Karol — the consecrated iron man — dies, Cardinal
> George Basil Hume will be elected Pope in England from where
> he travels unprotected except by prayer to an unsafe southern
> Europe without signing."

---

c	p	n	s	n	s	s	u	u	n	s	j	s	e	o	p	h
k	r	r	e	b	a	f	e	r	g	v	e	d	u	e	u	g
3	15	13	18	13	18	18	20	20	13	18	10	18	5	14	15	8
	17	17	5	2	1	6	5	17	7	21	5	4	20	5	20	7
3	6	4	9	4	9	9	2	2	4	9	1	9	5	5	6	8
	8	8	5	2	1	6	5	8	7	3	5	4	2	5	20	7
	9 Apr			4 Sep		Feb 2		Apr 9			195		2	Jun 8		
	Aug 8	95	Feb 1	96		May 0		2000		May 6			0	20 Jul		
						0							0			
						0							0			

A crucial period during 8 August 1995–9 April 1996 affects Pope John Paul II and consequently Cardinal George Basil Hume. Earlier, the Pope, or a situation influencing him, will be the subject of much prayer in southern Europe around 6 May 1995. Out of this troubled period, Cardinal Basil Hume, Archbishop of Westminster, is predicted to emerge as the next Pope.

Between 1 February–4 September 1996 he achieves a high profile in his new office, perhaps attempting to be a peacemaker in very dangerous circumstances.

In May–February 2000, he will be in England, but earlier in the year, around 9 April, he may have made a journey alone and unprotected, to pursue a new initiative for peace. However, he may make little progress throughout the year.

By 8 June–20 July 2000, he may secure a verbal agreement for peace.

This whole, uncertain period foreseen for his papacy may be related to turbulent social situations in southern Europe and Africa, as well as a war in the Middle East (see sections on NATIONS and 'General Colin Powell – Vice President').

Cardinal Hume, who has been head of the Roman Catholic Church in Britain since 1976. The opening of the new squash courts at Romford YMCA gave the cardinal a chance to show his talent for the game

December 1990 III.65

Civil Rights for British Witches

b   u
Cinq: en la Grande-Bretagne, petit à petit une maléfique
*   s   y*
peinture des sorcières fuit, en sort que le paganisme y est
*   m   m   f   q*
humanisé avec civiques droitures à don fructueux.

"1995 onwards: in Great Britain little by little a malefic picture of witches flies away, so that paganism there is humanised with civic rights. A fruitful gift."

PREDICTIONS for the next millennium show that in Britain we are going to become more adventurous and tolerant towards different forms of worship. This trend could result in a partial return to Britain's pagan past.

Paganism, based on veneration for nature and having survived underground during the centuries-long dominance of Christianity,

b	u	s	y	m	m	f	q
g	p	e	g	a	v	v	t
2	20	18	23	12	12	6	7
7	15	5	7	1	21	21	19
2	20	9	5	3	3	6	7
7	6	5	7	1	3	3	19
Feb	2		May	Mar	9		197
7	0						
	0	9			4	Mar	
	6	5	7				

A wave of interest in the old nature-worshipping religion of Pagan Europe will sweep over Britain and many countries on the continent

& will form one aspect of this new spiritual outlook. The 'Old Religion', as it is often called, will become officially recognised, with its worshippers being accorded civil rights in connection with the freedom to worship. Britain could be the first Western country to grant such rights.

The current view of witches (from 'Wicca', the name British pagans give to their religion) as evil, corrupting beings will gradually dissolve from 7 May 1995, perhaps in connection with a case before the European Courts.

Paganism is centred, not on a father god, but on a mother goddess whose attributes are visible through nature and the changing seasons. Many of its earth-caring principles have been taken up by ecologists since the sixties. During the next few years, pagans become, if not respectable, at least recognised, with the granting of rights during 9 March 1997–4 March 1998 to freedom from persecution, freedom to congregate and freedom to worship in their sacred places. Pagans do not enjoy any of these rights at present, an example being the prevention of access to Stonehenge at the time of the summer solstice.

Nostradamus considers that this change will ultimately prove of great benefit to British society by 7 February 2006, no doubt because many witches are reputed to possess psychic powers and this ability will soon become the subject of major scientific investigation.

February 1992 X.28

Reincarnation Becomes a Western Belief

x   v   u   t   f   t   h
Après l'an deux mille: désormais, la croyance à réincarnation
h   p   o   u   b   h   o   p   o
sied répandue à l'Ouest. En réponse, la perspective théologique
u   t   u   s   v   s
du christianisme a serpenté en fourrés.

"After the year 2000: from now on, belief in reincarnation becomes widespread in the West. In response, the theological perspective of Christianity has wandered into thickets."

A troubling prophecy with profound implications for Christianity over the next two decades.

The belief in reincarnation, a fundamental principle of Hinduism and Buddhism, has never found a place in Christian theology. However, with the decline of Christian influence in Western countries and the rise of secular societies, many people are today searching for an alternative spiritual philosophy.

In the next few years, Christian theology may feel itself to be under attack from scientific discovery and public questioning (1–5 October 1996 and 5 May 1997). The Church may not be able to rise to this new challenge, instead becoming embroiled from 4 March 1998 in 'thickets' of obscure arguments.

From 1 May 1998, a Western belief in reincarnation may begin steady growth.

Belief in reincarnation is immensely old. Many religions prior to the coming of Christianity had at their centre the process of birth, death and rebirth, supremely manifested in nature. Christianity, with its insistence that a particular man was resurrected from a state of death at a particular point in history contradicted what was then seen as the natural process. Early Christians often encountered prolonged outbreaks of extreme

x a	v a	u i	t i	f a	t y	h a	h d	p d	o a	u e	b n	h a	o i	p l	o d	u m	t a	u n	s n	v r	s
22	21	20	19	6	19	8	8	15	14	20	2	8	14	15	14	20	19	20	18	21	18
1	1	1:9	1:9	1	23	1	4	4	1	5	5	13	1	1:9	11	4	12	1	13	13	17
4	3	20	19	6	19	8	8	6	5	20	2	8	5	6	5	20	10	20	9	3	9
1	1	19	10	1	5	1	4	4	1	5	5	4	1	19	2	4	3	1	4	4	8

```
4Mar   2        196      198    8    Nov    2     Oct   5 196   May2   2    2009    Mar
       0                              0                               0   0            4  98
Jan 1  1    Oct 1   May 1  Aug        1     0    5    May          2    0    0    Jan 4
       0                         5                                      4    3
```

hostility precisely because this belief was viewed as an aberration of the natural process.

With its past insistence on treating the world as an obstacle course through which Christians must travel in order to gain heaven, the Church is now seen by many as lacking a great ecological statement at its heart. Christian countries, with their emphasis on economic growth and technology, are held responsible for endangering the delicate processes of the environment. Nor could it be argued that, had countries in Eastern Europe, now so ecologically devastated, remained free of Communism, they would have gone in a different direction. The benefits of technology are still seen to outweigh the disadvantages.

In the year 2003, the Christian Church may find itself boxed-in by its failure to stand by its original principles, encountering criticism both from faithful Christians and those outsiders who feel it has not gone far enough to meet their needs. It could begin modifying its theology to meet the latter growing challenge (2 May 2004).

Despite theological 'adjustments', public belief in reincarnation will be severely testing orthodox Christianity. By 1 August _8 November 2005 it may also be having a deepening effect on local and government policy in many countries. The reason is simple. If you believe you are destined to return to earth again and

A Hindu funeral in India. Hinduism is based on the constant recycling of lives which we call reincarnation

again, you will not want to find it an ecological wasteland where the quality and even the length of your life is severely restricted!

During 2009, the Church will try to appease two opposing sides, on the one hand, an increasingly fundamental Christianity and, on the other, the majority of people who seek fresh answers to their spiritual problems. This indecision could reach a height of unpopularity.

The final period is 1 January–4 March 2010. This may signify the final adoption by Christianity of reincarnation as one of its principal beliefs. Or it could herald the superseding of Christianity by a religion which possesses a belief in reincarnation.

It may even indicate the final, unchallengeable proof that reincarnation actually does occur.

June 1992 VII.14

NATO troops on exercise in Germany

WORLD
ORGANISATIONS

... as the world divides into economic power blocs ...

The Death of NATO

o   o   r   *f* *o*f   o
Cinq: l'aigle chauve fracassé force le décès de NATO. Amerique,

r   a   o   a
l'Europe parrainent un cadastre de l'aire de lancement. On

i   r   a
partage les bénéfices.

*"1995 onwards: the shattered bald eagle forces the death of
NATO. America and Europe sponsor a cadastral survey of the
eyrie's launching site. The benefits are shared."*

BY 1995 America – the 'bald eagle' – will find herself suffering from a devil's brew of predicted natural catastrophes mixed with continuing economic decline.

With huge domestic problems, she will cease to exercise a major foreign influence. One of the casualties of this policy will be NATO, formed after the Second World War to defend Western Europe against the Soviet empire in the East.

Following the East European revolutions in 1989, Soviet Communism finally collapsed after the failed coup of August 1991. Although NATO will endeavour to find a new role in Europe, America's decision to withdraw spells out a death sentence.

A huge logistical operation lasting for years is predicted, including the withdrawal of troops and civilian personnel and the disposal of missile sites and bases.

| o | o | r | f | o | f | o | r | a | o | a | i | r | a |
n	e	v	s	e	e	e	e	u	t	n	t	e	e
14	14	17	6	14	6	14	17	1	14	1	1:9	17	1
13	5	21	18	5	5	5	5	20	19	13	19	5	5
5	5	8	6	5	6	5	8	1	5	1	19	8	1
4	5	3	9	5	5	5	5	20	19	4	19	5	5
Oct		8	96	Nov		13		1	195	Jan		198	Jan
4		Aug						0					
					10		Oct	0		Apr		195	May
								2					

Following what appears to be a complete shutdown of the missiles and their launching pads from January–April 1995, America begins to pull back between 8 October 1996–4 August 1997 (significantly, presidential elections will take place in 1996 and this process may be accelerated by a new incumbent of the White House).

America and Europe will share the cost of a survey of the taxable land originally bought and leased by America to house her bases. This land, valued in billions of dollars, will be returned to the various countries to which it belongs, but will then have to be sold, or used for other purposes. Negotiations on the share-out of profits from this eventual sale may take place during May 1995–January 1998.

American military influence may not entirely disappear from Europe until 13 November 2001–10 October 2002. Perhaps this period also signifies the formation of a new European defence organisation based on the larger membership of a federal European Community after 2001.

March 1992 VIII.4

Third World Unites in Brazil

$$j \quad t \quad f \quad f \quad s \quad q$$
Après l'an deux mille, les pauvres pays du monde, nord et sud,
$$h \quad\quad h \quad d \quad s \quad s \quad t \quad s \quad i$$
forment une organisation nouvelle avec un bureau central en
$$s \quad s \quad e \quad t \quad c \quad s$$
Brésil. La citadelle germe par siècle.

"After the year 2000 the poor countries of the world, north and south, form a new organisation with its headquarters in Brazil. The citadel germinates throughout the world."

SINCE the end of the Second World War the gap in standards of living between the rich and poor countries has widened dramatically. People in the Third World suffer from poverty malnutrition and disease. In the main, they lack sophisticated education. They are less healthy and they die younger. This situation is likely to worsen before it improves.

Around 11 November 1995, the richer countries could withdraw into some kind of political and economic 'citadel' or fortress. A halt or reduction in overseas aid is implied, but the phrase also smacks of a stern measure of protectionism in which the poorer countries would lose out.

A year later, on 1 November 1996, the situation of the world's poor may be highlighted. These countries may decide to form a new association during 26 May–June 1997. Nations from both the northern and southern hemispheres would participate.

Between 13 February–2 April 1999, the new association could set up its headquarters in Brazil – evidence that South American countries will increasingly exercise influence on the world stage.

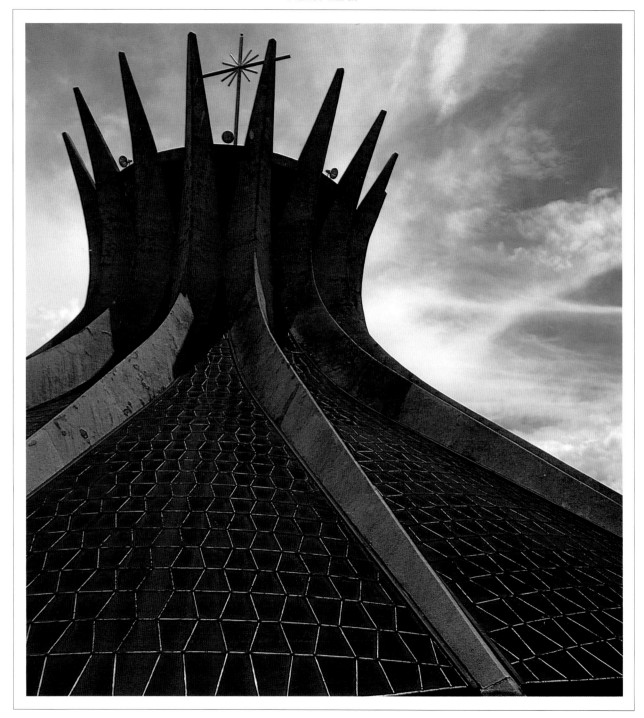

j l	t l	f a	f y	s n	q n	h o	h n	d v	s v	s n	t u	s n	i n	s b	s l	e l	t m	c p	s l
10	19	6	6	18	16	8	8	4	18	18	19	18	1:9	18	18	5	19	3	18
11	11	1	23	13	13	14	13	21	21	13	20	13	13	2	11	11	12	15	11
10	19	6	6	9	7	8	8	4	9	9	19	9	19	9	9	5	10	3	9
2	11	1	5	13	13	5	4	3	3	13	2	13	4	2	11	11	12	15	11
2	196	Jun	97		16	Apr	99		199		199				95			2003	Sep
0	Nov 1	May 26		May 23							Feb 13		Apr 2		Nov 11		Dec 26		
0																			
2																			

Once the world centre has been established, the new league will quickly formulate its structure, principles and policy between 23 May 1999–16 April 2000 – no doubt with an eye to the significance of a new millennium just beginning.

Between November 2002 and September 2003, the new organisation begins many projects whose success will ensure a future more hopeful than the past. Increased use of resources, reversal of ecological damage, culture and tourism may all play a part, but it is these countries which may leap from Third World status into advanced technological societies without ever passing through an industrial revolution. 26 December 2003 may be a significant date in this transition.

Siècle can also be translated as 'century' – indicating that this process is gradual and may last until the year 2100, when the present wide gulf between rich and poor could have disappeared completely.

Brasilia Cathedral

February 1993 II.51

Union for Asia–Pacific Nations

---

b   *b*   *r*   *g*   *x*   *d*
Cinq: le Japon forme liaisons intimes à l'Australie, coupés

b   *r*   *k*   *r*   *r*   *p*   *r r*   *r*
d'Amerique. Vers la Chine fait le guet stupéfait tandis que l'age

ſ   *r p*   *r*   *ſ*   *u*
passé prépare l'heure d'union grande.

"1995 onwards: Japan forms close links with Australia, both cut
off from America. Towards China she keeps an astonished watch
as the fading age prepares the hour of grand alliance."

THIS prediction, together with 'China in Revolution – Tibet
Freed' signals an astonishing turnaround in Chinese society
beginning from 1996. The period 17 June 1996–11 May
1997 witnesses the beginning of this transformation, the forerunner
of a grand alliance or union with her powerful neighbour Japan.

b	b	r	g	x	d	b	r	k	r	r	p	r	r	r	f	r	p	r	f	u
i	o	i	s	i	s	i	v	c	i	t	i	s	q	l	s	e	l	e	i	n
2	2	17	7	22	4	2	17	–	17	17	15	17	17	17	6	17	15	17	6	20
1:9	14	1:9	18	1:9	18	1:9	21	3	1:9	19	1:9	18	16	11	18	5	11	5	1:9	13
2	2	8	7	22	4	2	8	–	8	8	6	8	17	8	6	17	6	8	6	20
19	5	19	9	10	9	19	21	3	19	19	19	9	7	11	9	5	11	5	19	4
Feb 19 May	2	198	97		26 Feb Oct 28	Aug 21 Mar			198	198	196	98	17 Aug Jul 11	96		17 Jun May 11	Aug May	196		2 0 0 4

Marshy Island off the mouth of the River Sumida, with Yedo and Mount Fuji in the distance. Woodblock print by Ando Hiroshige c. 1857

Historic differences between these two nations make this outcome seem unlikely, but the prediction indicates that the imminence of the new millennium will be bearing down on these two countries, as it will on all of us, compelling them to respond to a much-changed world after the year 2000. To have an audible voice, each country will need to be involved in an economic power bloc, this situation eventually leading to world government.

Meanwhile, during 26 February–28 October 1997, Japan forges closer trading and economic links with Australia, both of them unable to carry on trade with America because of its own problems. The phrase 'both cut off from America' may be meant literally, since predictions of seismic movements along America's Pacific coast could affect airfields and ports for several years.

During 1998, Japan could be startled by China's rapid awakening into a dominant political and economic power in the East, perhaps overshadowing Japan just when she is experiencing acute difficulty. China is predicted to undergo a revolution leading to a democratic constitution.

Moves towards closer links will be initiated by Japan (2 February – 19 May 1998). These approaches may first be directed towards other countries with advanced economies in the Eastern Pacific – Taiwan and Malaya come to mind. 17 August could mark a formal approach or negotiation involving China. By 11 July 1999 awareness of an increasingly powerful European Community could lend urgency to the talks.

By 2004, a 'grand alliance' including Japan, China and other nations in the Asia–Pacific region, such as Australia and New Zealand, could be in place.

New Zealand man – will the Maoris and the Australian aborigines encounter difficulties in adjusting to union with Asian nations?

February 1993 III.53

European Parliament – World Government

d h   g   d   d d   x   u a
Cinq: le parlement européen devient le pouvoir réel de la
*   h a   u   a   a   u   o c*
Communauté. Il gouverne les membres nations — dix ans
*   d   a   c   a pa   o*
cacheront les germes d'autorité sur le monde.

"1995 onwards: the European parliament becomes the real power
of the Community. It governs the member nations — ten years
will conceal the seeds of authority over the world."

IN the ten years 1995–2005, the European parliament will grow in power and responsibility to become the nucleus of a world government. Many have speculated that the United Nations could eventually fulfil this role, but evidently this is not to be. One reason could be that the United States has put considerable funding into the activities of the UN, but may be reluctant to continue, with huge domestic problems troubling her.

The spark which sets off this crucially important European development occurs during 7 January–16 April 1995. Perhaps the parliament is thrust suddenly into major responsibility, or adverse circumstances may suddenly affect the UN.

During 8 April–16 May 1997, the parliament moves into the limelight, perhaps acquiring new powers. By 1 March 2000 the 'seeds' of its eventual world authority have been planted. It will have become the supreme governing body of the European Community by 24 May 2003–9 January 2004.

From 12 November 2004–1 January 2005, the parliament could become the governing authority for groups of nations outside the Community. Fifteenth June 2004 Marks a point when its transformation into a world government could be imminent.

The Lion of Waterloo, near Brussels

d	h	g	d	d	d	x	u	a	h	a	u	a	a	u	o	c	d	a	c	a	p	a	o
q	e	t	n	n	e	v	e	e	e	i	v	l	m	n	i	n	e	l	e	e	r	l	n
4	8	7	4	4	4	22	20	1	8	1	20	1	1	20	14	3	4	1	3	1	15	1	14
16	5	19	13	13	5	21	5	5	5	1:9	21	11	12	13	1:9	13	5	11	5	5	17	11	13
4	8	7	4	4	4	4	20	1	8	1	20	1	1	20	5	3	4	1	3	1	6	1	14
16	5	19	4	4	5	21	5	5	5	19	3	11	12	4	19	4	5	11		10		10	4
Apr	8197				12	Apr	2		9 Jan			2	1 Jan	2	2	195	7 Jan		Mar 1		Jun15		
16	May	Apr 30					0		May 24			0	Nov12	0		Apr 16			2000		2004		
							0					0		0									
							5					3		4									

By 30 April 2005–12 April 2006 the European Community, now consisting of many nations across the continent, may have become the dominant world power, the focus of global political organisation.

February 1993 IV.44

TRAVEL IN SPACE

... and people seek a new destiny in the galaxy ...

Space Station – Moon Landing Planned

b b g x db r hp h k
Cinq: une station européenne dans l'espace. À ce temps - là

r p r r r f r
l'énergie nucléaire sera transformé radicalement le plan

p r f j q
d'alunissage. Comprend un futur fulgurant.

"1995 onwards: a European space station. By that time nuclear energy will have revolutionised the plan for a moon landing. It encompasses a dazzling future."

| b | b | g | x | d | b | r | h | p | h | k | r | p | r | r | r | f | r | p | r | f | j | q |
c	n	n	n	s	l	c	a	c	e	l	l	c	e	n	n	e	l	s	m	n	t	n
2	2	7	22	4	2	17	8	15	8	–	17	15	17	17	17	6	17	15	17	6	10	16
3	13	13	13	18	11	3	1	3	5	11	11	3	5	13	13	5	11	18	12	13	19	13
2	2	7	4	4	2	8	8	15	8	–	8	6	8	8	8	6	8	6	17	6	10	7
3	13	4	4	9	11	3	1	3	5	11	2	3	5	4	13	5	2	9	12	13	10	4
Feb 13			94		Feb 98			15 Aug		2					30	Jun 2	96	17 Jun			2 Jul	
		24 Sep		11 Mar				Mar 16		0								Dec 13			0Apr	
										0						0					0	
										0	Mar 27					0					0	

Artist's impression of a space shuttle with a space construction facility. According to Nostradamus's prediction, such a project will soon move beyond the drawing board

NOSTRADAMUS has already predicted that during 1994, a European space station will become a serious project, especially during 13 February–24 September.

By 17 June–13 December 1996, it will be considered the first major step to a moon landing. During the next two years, plans for a long-term venture into space may be initiated. By February–11 March 1998, this could become a reality, based on new discoveries in physics and nuclear energy.

By 16 March–15 August 2000, new forms of energy will have dramatically transformed the prospects of going out into deep space, particularly during 27 March–30 June.

During July 2000–April 2001, humanity's dazzling future in space is seen to be assured.

September 1992 III.53

Moonbase to the Planets

Mars, photographed while in the constellation Taurus. The bright yellow star just below Mars is Aldebaran. The stellar cluster Pleiades can be seen to the upper right

      d *o*   *d* *h*   *d*   *o* *d*

Cinq: on construit une base sur la lune à loger des gens

      o   *d*   *h*   *o* *u*   *o*

nombreux. Devient l'aire de lancement aux planètes en premier

 c   *d*   *a* *c*   *a*   *a*   *o*

lieu, Mars. L'homme perdu à l'haute campagne.

"1995 onwards: a moonbase is built to house a large number of people. It becomes the launching site to the planets — in the first place, Mars. A man lost in the noble campaign."

THE section-by-section analysis suggests a somewhat different sequence of events from the main prediction, but the trends remain identical.

This whole project points to a Mars landing during the year 2000 to celebrate the new millennium. (Nostradamus has already predicted such a landing for that year.)

d	o	d	h	d	o	d	o	d	h	o	u	o	c	d	a	c	a	a	o
q	n	i	n	n	e	e	b	n	n	n	n	e	l	l	e	e	l	e	m
4	14	4	8	4	14	4	14	4	8	14	20	14	3	4	1	3	1	1	14
16	13	1:9	13	13	5	5	2	13	13	13	13	5	11	11	5	5	11	5	12
4	14	4	8	4	14	4	5	4	8	5	20	5	3	4	1	3	1	1	5
16	4	10	13	13	5	5	2	4	13	13	4	5	11	2	5	5	11	5	4
Apr	14	4	Aug	22		5		12 May			2	2	Mar 9						Jan
16 Apr		0		31 May		0	Apr	26			0	0			23 Nov				95
		0				0					0	0							
		2				2					4	0							

The prediction then 'jumps' to 23 November 2000–9 March 2001, the first landing having taken place earlier in the year. In this later period, there may have been further landings in which it is possible that a crewman will have lost his life.

During 14–16 April 2004, construction of a permanent Mars rocket base could begin or be completed. During 26 April – 12 May, a major decision may be taken to make this base the main site for launching expeditions to other planets in the solar system. This year may see the beginning of such expeditions.

By 22 August 2005–31 May 2006, a base housing a large number of people could also be sited on the moon.

Earth Conquers the Solar System

q   b   r   m   q

Après l'an deux mille, les astronautes voyagent en éspace en

f   i   i   q   u   d u d

vaisseaux que ressemblent aux cités. Font tenir à la système

u   m   i   i   q

externe, huit à circonférence. Puis dur fuit.

"After the year 2000, astronauts travel in space in ships resembling cities. They hold the outer system, eight to the circumference. Then the tough one flies."

Space stations like the one depicted here could be operative early in the next millennium

A leap back in time: the
medieval view of the
universe. Man looks
from his world into the
Cosmos

BETWEEN 2004–2007, hundreds or even thousands of human beings will voyage in space ships resembling cities to all the planets in the solar system, except the ninth, Pluto, which is so far away that it takes 248 years to orbit the sun.

At first sight this statement seems unbelievable, since 2007 is less than fifteen years away and we have yet to make a successful trip to any of our planetary neighbours.

However, a predicted enormous acceleration in scientific knowledge and the application of new space technology will prove to be unstoppable, with humanity all but conquering the solar system in the first few years of the millennium.

Earth scientists and technicians will develop a method of travelling to the planets using tremendous speeds.

Section Two of the dating display not only confirms the eight planets again, but also repeats the period of 2004–2007. If we understand the first 3 in the equation to be the planet Earth, the third planet from the sun, then the other numbers in the section may indicate a record of the first journeys from Earth to its neighbours.

q	b	r	m	q	f	i	i	q	u	d	u	d	u	m	i	i	q
x	l	v	n	a	v	e	l	x	s	a	l	s	x	a	e	s	t
16	2	17	12	16	6	1:9	1:9	16	20	4	20	4	20	12	1:9	1:9	16
22	11	21	13	1	21	5	11	22	18	1	11	18	22	1	5	18	19
7	2	8	3	7	6	10	10	7	2	4	2	4	2	3	10	10	7
4	2	3	4	1	3	5	2	4	9	1	2	9	4	1	5	9	10
2007			8(planets)			2	2	July	2	Apr	2	Apr	2	Mar	2	2	2
2004			3 + 7 +6			0	0		0		0		0		0	0	0
			+20 = 1 + 3			0	0	4	0	1	0	9	0	1	0	0	0
			= 2000 + 4			5	2	9		2		4			5	9	7
			= 2004 + 3														
			= 2007														

By 2005, huge ships are already travelling in deep space, the first successful flights with this type of craft having begun around 1 April 2002.

Between 9 April 2004–1 March 2005, projects will be set up for flights to begin to the outer planets – Saturn, Uranus, Neptune.

After 2007, only Pluto is left to overcome on a final long haul around the date 4 July 2009, with Nostradamus hinting that it could be a difficult journey.

There is an alternative interpretation.

Nostradamus could also be hinting at the discovery of a *tenth* planet for the simple reason that astronauts do not need to voyage to Earth – they already live there. So the phrase 'eight to the circumference' could possibly exclude Earth and include Pluto.

If so, then the 'long haul' in 2009 might be targeted on a tenth planet, moving far out in space and as yet unknown to us.

September 1991 X.89

Mars – A Sensational Discovery

h   m d d   c

Après l'an deux mille une expédition à la planète Mars trouve

     a   u   o   c d   c

des stries en losanges, doublées d'appareil et gorgées d'eau. Un

       m   o

mouchard rapproché, à touche mou.

"After the year two thousand an expedition to the planet Mars finds some diamond-shaped ridges, lined with apparatus and filled with water. A control device nearby, with a soft touch."

AROUND 8 June 2003, a surveying expedition could land on Mars, equipped for a stay of several years, although the original team may be enlarged by further arrivals during the next two years. One of the expedition's main responsibilities will be a survey of 'the red planet' before preparing a detailed map.

h	m	d	d	c	a	u	o	c	d	c	m	o
p	l	e	e	p	s	s	l	e	e	n	p	e
8	12	4	4	3	1	20	14	3	4	3	12	14
15	11	5	5	15	18	18	11	5	5	13	15	5
8	3	4	4	3	1	20	5	3	4	3	3	5
6	2	5	5	6	9	9	2	5	5	4	6	5
8	3	Dec					2005	3	Apr	Jun		5
Jun	0											
	0				25	Nov	10				2005	
	2											

The surface of Mars showing the landslides in Phir Chasm, which lies in the centre of the giant Martian canyon system, the Valles Marineris. In just such a desolate area, evidence of alien civilisation may be found

On or after Christmas Day the expedition will locate a group of 'diamond-shaped ridges', possibly identified at first as nothing more than an unusual geological formation. This would explain the interval of eighteen months before the ridges are investigated – they are just one in many thousands of sites being mapped.

It appears that there are several of these ridges, each one shaped like a diamond, not a set of ridges making one diamond.

Not until after 3 April 2005 is the sensational discovery made that the 'diamonds' contain water and that their sides are lined with some kind of apparatus, much of it below the water level.

In other words, they are artificial reservoirs.

The implications of such a discovery would be mind-blowing, for there are really only two explanations. One is that these are relics of a long-lost Martian civilisation which died out when the air became too rarefied. The other is that this installation is a way-station for visiting alien spaceships. The second explanation seems more likely, given another prediction in this book which suggests that our galaxy is teeming with alien life-forms (See 'Sounds from the Stars').

A second consideration is that the 'machinery' may extract water from deep within the planet. There has been much speculation that Mars has reserves of water trapped beneath the surface.

The 'apparatus' must also keep the water fresh.

This discovery may represent a breakthrough in technology for irrigating the ever-increasing desert areas back on earth. Is it possible that we shall use alien technology to provide an environmental solution to this relentless advance?

Finally, the device controlling the apparatus will be found 'nearby' around 5 June 2005. 'A soft touch' may mean that it is activated by varying degrees of fingertip pressure, like a highly sensitive computer keyboard, or the phrase could describe the alien material from which the device is made as being 'soft' to the touch.

June 1992 IV.44

Hostile Venus Colonised

g   *P*   *g*
Après l'an deux mille, une colonie, que se suffit à soi-méme,
         b   *g*   *r*
qu'on doit se tapir des buées baroques, turbulentes de
   r   *r*   *b*   *r*   *u*   *r*   *c*   *q*
l'atmosphère de la planète barbare, Vénus. Tache de tarder
     u
l'attaque.

"After the year 2000, a self-supporting colony that must be hidden from the weird, turbulent atmospheric vapours of the barbarous planet, Venus. It tries to delay the onslaught."

NOSTRADAMUS predicts that, during the first decade of the new millennium, human beings will have travelled to nearly all the planets in the solar system. One of these stopping-places will be Venus.

Scientific descriptions of this planet call up visions of Dante's hell. From satellite photos and scientific tests we know that the greenhouse effect has run wild on Venus, its rich carbon dioxide clouds trapping the sun's heat and sending surface temperatures up to 800 degrees Centigrade. The atmospheric pressure is 90 times that of Earth, while the 'rain' that falls from the clouds is sulphuric acid.

Nevertheless, as early as the year 2000, a project may be initiated with the aim of installing a fully self-sufficient colony on the planet. The final decision could be taken between 13 July 2000–14 April 2001. The reason may lie in the fact that, although Venus is roughly the same size and age as Earth, something has gone terribly wrong with its atmosphere. By 2000, we may have become worried enough about our own atmosphere, rapidly altering under the effects of pollution, to find out more about that of Venus.

Radar image of the surface of Venus, showing the Lakshmi region. This type of terrain has not been seen previously, either on Venus or the other planets. The fainter set of parallel lineations are spaced at regular intervals of about 1 kilometre

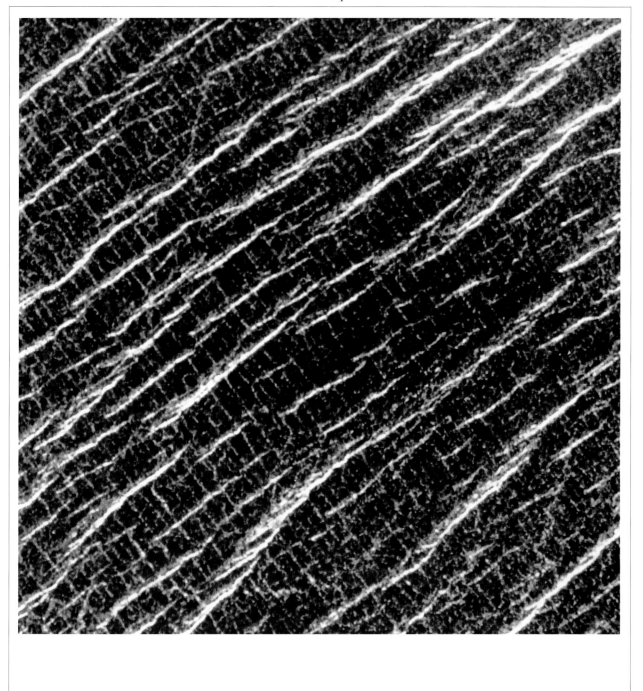

g	p	g	b	g	r	r	r	b	r	u	r	c	q	u
n	e	s	e	e	e	o	d	n	a	e	h	d	d	a
7	15	7	2	7	17	17	17	2	17	20	17	3	16	20
13	5	18	5	5	5	14	4	13	1	5	8	4	4	1
7	6	7	2	7	8	8	8	2	8	20	8	3	7	20
4	5	9	5	5	5	5	4	4	1	5	8	4	4	1
	13	Jul		2007		16	Aug	2	Aug	2	8		Oct	2
Apr 14			May 5					0		0				0
					May 9			0		1	0	Dec	4	0
								4		5				1

The phrase 'it tries to delay the onslaught' seems to refer to the intense preparations and research designed to prevent the colony being immediately overwhelmed by the poisonous and unpredictable atmospheric system on Venus. Solutions may consist of a sealed dome, or perhaps an electromagnetic force field, or even technology which has not yet been invented (4 October 2001).

The colony could begin to function between 9 May 2004–16 August 2005, with settlement being established towards the end of this period, around 1 August.

Despite immense difficulty, the colony is still there two years later when, from 5 May, the inhabitants, mostly scientists and engineers, may begin to discover weird powers or effects connected with the chemical vapours making up the planet's atmosphere.

May 1992 I.28

Sounds from the Stars

HUGE radio telescopes on earth are already scanning the heavens for signs of communication from intelligent extra terrestrial life. It seems that their efforts may begin to be rewarded by the end of this decade.

---

   f   *h*   *c*
Après l'an deux mille on décèle souvent sons purs de la vie
      f *c*   *p*   *h*
extra-terrestre que voyagent des étoiles à la terre. On a besoin
p *h* *c*   *h* *p*   *u*
d'opérer la poursuite choisie. Nus pour muets.

"After the year 2000, pure sounds of extra-terrestrial life are often detected, travelling from the stars to earth. It is necessary to operate a carefully chosen pursuit. (The sounds) revealed for the silent."

---

f	h	c	f	c	p	h	p	h	c	h	p	u
a	l	d	y	d	l	a	d	e	a	e	e	e
6	8	3	6	3	15	8	15	8	3	8	15	20
1	11	4	23	4	11	1	4	5	1	5	5	5
6	8	3	6	3	6	8	6	8	3	8	6	20
1	2	4	5	4	2	1	4	5	1	5	5	5
Jun	8				99	Aug	14			11	Jun	2
1	Feb	Sept		6				10	Jan	10		0
												0
												5

The Very Large Array (VLA) radio telescope near Socorro, New Mexico. The VLA consists of 27 dish antennae, each one 25 metres in diameter, positioned along the arms of a 21 x 19km Y-shaped railway network. A computer combines the data from the 27 antennae, so that in effect they form one single giant radio dish

What may be the first-ever artificial signals from outer space to be detected by us will be received on or after 6 September 1999.

During 8 February–1 June 2000 two things may happen. Firstly, the signals may be verified as having an artificial source, meaning that only intelligent life could have transmitted them. Secondly, whereas previously the signals may have been distorted by 'background noise' coming from natural activity within the universe itself, a method will be discovered to isolate the sounds so that they are heard by us in a pure form, just as they were transmitted.

By 14 August 2000, an operation will have been set up to receive and analyse the signals. Nostradamus warns that selection is very necessary when locating them. Perhaps this is because, by this time, we may have detected signals from more than one source.

It is one thing to hear these sounds and quite another to know what they mean. The last fascinating phrase suggests that by 10 January–11 June 2005, we may have begun to decode and understand the signals. In fact, they may have been despatched for that purpose, just as we have sent out information about ourselves in probes or in radio transmissions. These sounds may constitute our first 'lesson' about intelligent life elsewhere in the universe.

March 1992 VII.14

THE NEW AGE

... and the long divide between spiritual and physical end

France Honours Nostradamus

> *a l   u   a*
> La France sent poinçon rusé en les prophèties des Siècles. Ouvre
> *j   p   p   u   g   u   a   g*
> un foyer pour le monde où penseur fait quête — l'héritage de
> *n   s   n   s*
> Nostradamus sera l'avenir.

> "France becomes aware of the cunning engraver's mark in the
> prophecies of the Centuries. She opens a centre of learning for
> the world where the thinker can search — the heritage of
> Nostradamus will be the future."

a n	l p	u t	a s	j f	p o	p e	u f	g t	u l	a t	g e	n t	s e	n l	s i
1	11	20	1	10	15	15	20	7	20	1	7	13	18	13	18
13	15	19	18	6	14	5	6	19	11	19	5	19	5	11	1:9
1	2	20	1	10	6	6	20	7	20	1	7	4	9	4	9
4	6	10	9	6	5	5	6	10	2	10	5	10	5	11	19
1	Feb	2		17	Jun	2	Jul	2	Jan 7		Apr 9		Apr	199	
Apr	6	0	Sep 16			0	Oct	0	2005		2005		Nov		
		1				0		0							
		0				6		2							

MICHAEL NOSTRADAMVS,
San - Remigius,
Præftantissimus sui temporis Mathematicus et
Henrico II. Galliarum Regi diem fatalem praedixit.
Natus A. 1494.   *Den. A. 1566. d. 2 Iulij, æt. 72.*
G.W. knor. sc. Nor.

AS France honours Nostradamus, so he will honour her among other nations.

During April –November 1999, the desire many people to know the future will become an issue of national importance in France, the country of Nostradamus.

Between October 2002 –July 2003, various initiatives may be proposed, but it is not until 7 January–9 April 2005 that a permanent design may emerge for preserving the heritage of Nostradamus.

During 16 September 2006–17 June 2007, a world centre will open for the study of *Siècles*, the prophetic work of Nostradamus.

Between 6 April 2010–1 February 2011, France may make a brilliant discovery about the prophetic code.

December 1991 III.65

Television Powers the Mind

Après l'an deux mille le monde de la télévision ouvre une porte aux pouvoirs de l'ésprit. Use une combinaison de physique et anticipation d'ère future. C'est source d'or.

"After the year 2000, the world of television opens a door to the powers of the mind. It uses a combination of physics and anticipation of the future age. A golden source."

THE activity described, although linked with 'the world of television', seems to be unknown at present, but may relate to Altered State technology, now in its infancy.

'Altered State' or 'brain health' refers to technology designed to produce advanced relaxation techniques that also promise enhanced creativity, concentrated mental energy and the possibility of treating stressful or violent mental conditions. The most widely used systems usually consist of a headset which introduces the user to a range of flickering lights producing visual images. Changes in brainwave patterns result. Music therapy could also be part of this treatment.

This new technology, which the viewer can mentally 'step into', has a real, but unexpected, impact from 2 March 2000 – possibly from a chance discovery.

Further experiments may open a door to formidable 'powers' during 5 May–16 August. Possibilities could include increasing a person's IQ and treatment of mental stress, or certain mental illnesses. These powers could have a psychic aspect.

The discovery is translated into television technology by 7 April 2006, to which the ordinary consumer will have access.

During 17 September 2008–9 March 2009, new knowledge of physics (possibly arising from new theories concerning time) could be combined with this technology, stretching the mind's capacities even further.

By 14 September 2009–6 April 2010, the hunt is on to produce a new Nostradamus – or perhaps many, because this technology could begin to release a power dormant in all of us to predict the future.

These discoveries promise immense mental and physical benefits to society.

Television viewing in the fifties. Argument has raged over whether it influences the mind for good or evil. This medium will acquire even greater powers over thought in the next decade

October 1991 VII.14

g	p	h	r	h	t	f	c	h	s	h	s	s	p	r	s
d	i	e	n	a	i	d	l	i	m	d	y	i	d	u	d
7	15	8	17	8	19	6	3	8	18	8	18	18	15	17	18
4	1:9	5	13	1	1:9	4	11	1:9	12	4	23	1:9	4	20	4
7	6	8	8	8	10	6	3	8	9	8	9	9	6	8	9
4	10	5	4	1	10	4	2	10	3	4	5	10	4	2	4
7	6		16	Aug	2	2	Mar	8		17	Sep	9		14	Sep
Apr	0	May	5		0	0	2	0	Mar	9		0	Apr	6	
	0				0	0		0				0			
	2				0	0		2				2			

Talking to Dolphins – A Breakthrough

g   o   ʃ
Après l'an deux mille on s'escrime à comprendre via phonétique
p b   o   p o   u   t
la parole des dauphins, sauvés de mers toxiques que tuent les
u   r   t
thons; or succès vient par chercher flots.

*"After the year 2000, there is a hard effort to understand via
phonetics the speech of dolphins saved from toxic seas that kill
tuna fish; but success comes through searching for waves."*

HUMAN beings are a lonely species, intensely aware that they are set apart from other animals. The need to regain a lost understanding with other species is great — hence the general fascination with the possibility of meeting extra-ter-restrials.

The prediction begins during 7 March–2 June 1995, following a discovery that poisonous waste in the earth's seas is killing tuna fish in large numbers. A decision will be taken to rescue dolphins from the same fate. Dolphins often swim with schools of tuna and have been accused of depleting stocks, but by 1995, it is clear that toxic chemicals in the water are responsible.

The scale of this operation cannot be judged. Perhaps only a few dolphins are selected to breed in a controlled environment which approximates as closely as possible to the wild state. However, the project may be much larger, engaged in by many countries.

Between 1997–2001 a project is set up to try and decipher the rapid, clicking language of these 'resident' dolphins. They are highly intelligent with brains larger than ours and many trained dolphins have been able to understand over a hundred words of English, while we still cannot get to grips with theirs. Doubts have been expressed as to whether it is a language at all. This sit-uation, the prediction asserts, will change.

Dolphins in the Pacific, perhaps a sight not available to the camera for much longer

g	o	f	p	b	o	p	o	u	t	u	r	t
a	l	m	d	d	a	d	m	q	q	a	c	s
7	14	6	15	2	14	15	14	20	19	20	17	19
1	11	12	4	4	1	4	12	16	16	1	3	18
7	5	6	6	2	5	6	5	20	19	20	8	19
1	2	3	4	4	1	4	3	7	7	1	3	9
7	95		Jun	2	95	6	May	2		2	Aug	
	Mar					Apr	3	0		0		
								0	197	0	3	199
								7		1		

A breakthrough occurs around 3 August 1999.

At first, the project team will have devoted their efforts to breaking down the 'clicks' phonetically by trying to attribute a separate meaning to each sound the dolphin makes. This approach fails. 'Success comes through searching for waves' may indicate that dolphin speech is very rhythmic and that it is these rhythms and the analysis of sounds occurring with each rhythm that produce the breakthrough.

Dolphins have a highly developed sonar system. They also swim fast through waves just beneath the water's surface. Perhaps there is a connection here.

By 3 April–6 May 2007, we may be engaged in a rewarding two-way communication with these talkative dolphins, by then unable to return to their native habitat because the poisonous seas would kill them too.

Political Rights for Animals

g   y   j   q f   p   c   p   p
Après l'an deux mille, les droits des animaux seront une partie

q   s   s   s   b
de la culture nouvelle. Errent. Soin fonctionnera à l'échelon

s   s   r   o   r   r
ministériel. Peu de temps avant un four un tueur fou.

"*After the year 2000, animal rights will be a part of the new culture. They wander about. Care will function at the ministerial level. Only a little time before the oven, mad killer.*"

A new respect for the rights of animals will strongly feature in the culture of the new millennium, particularly during 2 January–7 May 2004.

This new attitude may be enshrined in political legislation by 6 July 2006–2 February 2007. New laws could impose minimum principles of care for domesticated animals, including the requirement for all farming to be freerange, and the ending of experimental research using animals, together with any form of hunting or catching animals for sport.

The earlier date 3 April 2006 may signify a referendum or official recognition that humanity cannot continue to ignore the natural rights of other creatures.

By 16 June 2009–2 February 2010, this new attitude may be so deeply engrained that it results in a Bill of Rights for all creatures, one of its clauses giving animals unrestricted freedom to wander where they choose. How this will work in practice is not clear.

Between 2 September 2009–1 February 2010, this will become an important issue at government level and we may see Ministers for Animal Welfare being appointed in many administrations.

g	y	j	q	f	p	c	p	p	q	s	s	s	b	s	s	r	o	r	r
a	l	x	l	l	i	x	t	a	a	l	i	a	l	i	d	m	a	u	u
7	23	10	16	6	15	3	15	15	16	18	18	18	2	18	18	17	14	17	17
1	11	22	11	11	1:9	22	19	1	1	11	1:9	1	11	1:9	4	12	1	20	20
7	5	10	7	6	6	3	6	6	7	9	9	9	2	9	9	8	5	8	8
1	2	4	2	2	10	4	10	1	1	2	10	1	2	10	4	3	1	2	2

```
7 May   2   Jul 6   6   3   6   Jun 16       9   Sep 2   9   Sep 29
Jan 2   0   2 Feb   0   Apr 0       2   Feb 0   1 Feb   0               2000   Feb
        0       0       0               0       0
        4       2       2               2       2
```

The final phrase is extraordinary. It suggests the rise of an extreme, militant vegetarianism at the beginning of the millennium. Just as smokers nowadays are rapidly becoming social pariahs, so people who still cook and eat meat will be reviled, regarded as 'mad killers'.

Nostradamus says this change occurs only a little while after February–29 September 2000, so it could be the motivating force for all later developments.

Donkey sanctuaries could be the harbinger of a new era for the rights of animals

January 1992 IX.36

Physical Universe – Spiritual World

f   t   f   x   r   a
Cinq: le savoir nouvel du quantum mène à la croyance que le
* g   r a   f   r   u   c   t*
monde spirituel est une dimension invisible, sans Espace-Temps,
t   t f   q   u
de l'univers physique. Ténèbres et lumière une seule.

*"1995 onwards: new knowledge about the quantum leads to the
belief that the spiritual world is an invisible dimension, without
Space-Time, of the physical universe. Darkness and light are
one."*

'...F OR then we would know the mind of God'.
With these now famous words Stephen
Hawking ends his book *A Brief History of Time*. A
unifying theory of the universe, he says, would explain why we
and the universe exist. This prediction suggests that the revelation is very near.

The prediction forecasts a coming together of physical science
and spiritual philosophy early in the next century. The nearer the
twin sciences of astronomy and physics get to an explanation of
the origin of the universe, the closer that union approaches.
From 15 March 1996, we may have a much clearer picture of
the nature of the universe, perhaps through a new theory or
some discovery coming from a galaxy an unimaginable distance
away in space and time.

Excitement over the implications of this discovery could grow
so that, by 14 March 2000–14 January 2001, a strong conviction
exists that the spiritual world – Heaven, Paradise, the abode of
the dead, call it what you will – is a real though invisible
dimension of the universe that we see. This belief is strengthened
by theories relating to quantum theory which lead to a new
understanding of time.

The mushroom cloud of water and radioactive material produced by the test detonator of an atomic bomb at Bikini Atoll on the Pacific Marshall Islands, on 25 July 1946

Quantum mechanics describe the mysterious world in which nucleus and circling electrons live in the lonely space of the atom. It is the science of the incredibly small, the basic building-bricks of the universe, whereas Einstein's theory of relativity describes the workings of the huge structures in the universe – galaxies, star systems, planets. These two theories – quantum and relativity – would, once reconciled, provide a unifying theory of how the universe works. But at the moment this is impossible to do, although the situation is predicted to alter within the next ten years.

For April–July 2002 we have the mysterious phrase 'darkness and light are one'. Here we see a mystical note entering the prediction.

If we go back one stage to the linking of quantum theory and time, I believe that this whole thing may be about the Big Bang. Observations have proved that the universe is expanding; galaxies are moving away from us. Reverse that process in time to some twenty thousand million years ago and you have the creation of the universe from a single point, incredibly dense, without Space-Time, since this could only come into existence after the universe began expanding.

The next question is, naturally, *what happened before the Big Bang?* To which the answer is that since time did not exist at that point, there was no 'before'. This is unsatisfactory. You cannot instruct a whole civilisation of people in the linear concept of cause, effect and result in all aspects of their lives and then tell them that on the biggest topic of all – the making of the universe – there appears to have been no cause, only effect and possibly a result, though we won't be around to see what it is. Something is missing.

'Darkness and light are one' could refer to another unexplained phenomenon – the existence of 'dark matter'. For some years scientists have realised that, for galaxies and other formations to retain their structure, the universe must be ten to a hundred times bigger than the physical universe which we can detect with our instruments. This invisible 'dark matter' must be present, otherwise galaxies would break up and go flying off in all directions. The gravitational pressure of the dark matter prevents this.

f	t	f	x	r	a	g	r	a	f	r	u	c	t	t	t	f	q	u
v	v	m	n	l	l	e	l	s	o	v	n	e	s	l	v	p	n	l
6	19	6	22	17	1	7	17	1	6	17	20	3	19	19	19	6	16	20
21	21	12	13	11	11	5	11	18	14	21	13	5	18	11	21	15	13	11
6	10		10	10	1	7	10	1	6	8	20	3	10	10	19	6	7	20
3	3	12	13		11	5		9	5	3	4	5	9	11	3	15	4	2
Jun	2	2000	2		Jan	7	2	Jan	14			2003	2000			196	Jul	2
Mar	0	Dec 13	0	11	May		0	14	Mar	Apr	5		Sep	11	Mar	15		0
	0		0			0											Apr	
	3		0			0												2

But what if this 'dark matter' were not 'dark' at all, but 'light?'

I believe this is what the prediction is telling us. The vast mass of the universe is moving beyond the speed of light, at a velocity at which it becomes undetectable or invisible to creatures of this universe. This unseen dimension would be all around us, perhaps able to move through physical matter itself, but because it would be travelling at many times the speed of light, it would be impossible to detect – at least with the technology we possess now. We may be living in only a fragment of this vast universe.

So what happened *before* the Big Bang? Perhaps a piece of this 'light universe' became detached in some cataclysm and began slowing down through the levels of lightspeed until it coalesced into our universe. The latest theories about the Big Bang suggest that the expansion of the universe took place at many times the speed of light in an instant of time – suppose this were not a speeding up, but a *slowing down*? The vital spark entered this dimension at an unimaginable velocity and was then transformed in a moment of time into star-creating energy.

It then went on to create life which, for the most part, could not detect that other, light universe.

I say 'for the most part', because human beings have always associated light with a spiritual or divine revelation. And, of course, innumerable mystics down the ages would have us believe that they have special gifts that detect aspects of this spiritual world, or dimension.

The final dating, March–June 2003, indicates that knowledge about this subject hardens at this point. 5 April may mark an explanation of how this 'light universe' operates without the concept of Space-Time, possibly a steadystate existence – in other words, the eternal 'Now', or eternity.

February 1993 X.89

Proof of Life After Death

g h   s   c   c   h
Après l'an deux mille spiritisme soutient la croyance à la vie
p   h   p   c   h
après mort. Subit le réseau sophistiqué ouvre une porte entre
*   o   p   u e s*
deux mondes, or on se vérifie. Fin à doute.

"*After the year 2000 spiritualism confirms belief in life after death. Suddenly, the sophisticated network opens up a gateway between two worlds, now it is proved. An end to doubt.*"

A strange prediction, made eerie by the certainty with which it asserts that, within a few years, we shall receive absolute proof that the human personality survives death.

In fact, part of this proof may rest on the accuracy of the work I am doing, for if it can be proved that a man can leave his body and go roaming centuries into the future, then consciousness is not a by-product of the brain's activity, but a separate entity altogether.

During this decade public discussion of issues of life and death combined with worldwide events may cause spiritualism — the attempt to contact and communicate with the dead — to assert itself in a new way. People normally seek out a spiritualist when they are in despair at having lost a loved one and need to know they still exist somewhere.

The sheer scale of human tragedy across many countries, to which no politician or churchman will be able to supply satisfactory answers, will drive many previous doubters to seek out spiritualism for the first time. Spiritualism's new significance could emerge during 4 April–7 August 1995, when a long-term project to investigate personal survival may begin.

| g | h | s | c | c | h | p | h | p | c | h | o | p | u | e | s |
n	d	e	i	i	y	a	m	e	a	i	m	i	i	a	d
7	8	18	3	3	8	15	8	15	3	8	14	15	20	5	18
13	4	5	1:9	1:9	23	1	12	5	1	1:9	12	1:9	1:9	1	4
7	8	9	3	3	8	15	8	6	3	8	5	6	20	5	9
4	4	5	10	10	5	1	3	5	1	19	3	10	10	1	4
7	Aug		3	3		23	Aug	Jun	3	198	May	6	2	May	9
Apr	4	95	0	0	May	4		5	Jan		Mar	0	0	1	Apr
			0	0								0	1		
			2	2								2	0		

Monument to Juliana, Countess of Leicester, Holkam church, Norfolk

Spiritualism, rapidly becoming a revitalised force in society, may reorganise itself at this time to meet the growing demand for knowledge of 'the other side'.

3 June 1998–5 January 1999 marks a turningpoint when proof of personality survival is offered. As a result, a permanent gateway of communication is rapidly opened up between this world and the next. The prediction stresses the suddenness of this development.

Organisation becomes much more sophisticated through the creation of a new network, possibly initiated, even, by those of the other side of the created 'entrance'. Some extra ingredient may be included in 'sophisticated network'. Does it reflect innovative technology, or perhaps new scientific thinking about the nature of the universe? Either way, it produces a great leap forward.

Throughout 2003, spiritualism may be hitting the headlines. In particular, during 23 August 2003–4 May 2004, belief in life after death may be strengthened by a series of proofs. From March–May 2006 a permanent 'channel' may open between two worlds, with increasing confirmation of profound truths.

Whether this advance is technical or spiritual, or a combination of both, the research will progress at a furious pace so that, by 1 April–9 May 2010, all doubt about personality survival after death will end.

July 1992 VII.14

CHAPTER 3:

THE KEY TO THE CENTURIES

MY approach to understanding the prophecies of Nostradamus is different from all others.

Because it *is* so different, what I have to say will often be challenged by those who have difficulty in accepting its implications. Such critics are many. Emotionally, I number myself among them, because my instinct, too, is to reject it out of hand. The method's saving grace is that it appears to work.

I argue that, to understand his prophecies, you have to ignore their outward form and, using the system explained in this book, dismantle them to find the true prophecies concealed beneath.

The theory is controversial because it has always been accepted practice to interpret, as they were written, the distorted prophecies which were first published in the form that we know them in 1568. The incoherent form was all that anyone had to go on. That was why interpretations have always been inconclusive – every writer could find a different one for each verse, but none of them could be proved because there was no consistent, logical system for doing so.

Yet, although towards the end of his life he burned all his private papers that might have helped others to understand what he had done, Nostradamus did leave definite hints and clues.

In the Preface to his prophecies, he tells us that they are the twisted, obscure form of his original predictions because *these* were too astonishing to set before the people of his time. In plain terms, they would not have known what he was talking about.

Nostradamus lived in the sixteenth century during the period of the Reformation and the Renaissance. Both developments, together with the opening up of vast territories in America and, later, Australasia, would profoundly alter human society. Over the past four centuries, people all over the world have been caught up in a whirlwind of change. They have witnessed a decline in the political power of the Christian Church and the concept of monarchy, the rise of democracies, the ascendancy and now the fall of Communism.

Above all, they have, every one of them, been deeply affected by an ever-accelerating range of scientific discoveries and new technologies. Lives have been devastated or immensely enriched by the same remorseless advance.

We are not the people we were. If Nostradamus knew this sufficiently to wish to conceal the chasm of experience dividing his own generation from those to come, would he not have gone to extraordinary lengths to prove that here, thrust out of the past, was a shield to protect our uncertain progress into the future?

Fortunately, he has left us such proof – first of all, in the curious title of his great prophetic work.

Siècles means 'centuries' or 'cycles'. In this book we have seen how the same prophecies can be made to 'move' from one century to another by the use of date codes.

As for 'cycles' or 'something that goes round', the dating system for each new prediction is divided into sections that move either clockwise or anticlockwise.

But is there something more in this vague title than at first appears? Yes, if we apply the principles of decoding.

s

Siècles = sien clé   'his key'

Consider what this means.

All along, in the title of his book for over 400 years, has lain concealed a clue to the opening up of the prophecies, those strange, mystical quatrains which have puzzled countless readers.

This is Nostradamus' own chosen title for his work – not 'centuries', not 'cycles', but the true, extended name:

SIÈCLES – SIEN CLÉ,
THE CENTURIES – HIS KEY

Why did he choose this title? Because the Great Work which he undertook was the teaching all over again of prophecy and the knowledge it can bring to a society which had cut itself off completely from that knowledge. How would he do this marvellous thing? By constructing a great literary 'mechanism' consisting of hundreds of prophecies, each one an independent predictive device, a machine whose very bulk would enable it to survive unrecognised for what it was through four centuries of questioning and doubt. This is *his* key to the centuries ahead, his legacy to our generation and those who come after us. It opens the door to our future.

s	18
Siècles = sien clé	13

It has a dating device, this title, expressing secret information connected with Nostradamus' own life and work. The device can be understood in three ways.

s = 18
n = 13

$$18 - 13 = 5$$
$$18 + 13 = 31$$

The year (1)531 has emerged. So now *Siècles* means:

The Centuries – His Key – 1531,

In 1531, Nostradamus was still a young man, less than thirty. His first published predictions, in the form of an almanac, would not appear until 1550. Nevertheless, there has to be a fact of such great significance connected with the year 1531 that Nostradamus decided to conceal it in the secret title of his prophecies.

I believe the device is telling us that it was in 1531 that Nostradamus began secretly to write down his master work of prophecy, almost two decades before he began publishing his almanacs. It would be a further five years before the first collection of prophecies under the title of *Siècles* would appear, in 1555. If, as seems likely, he went on writing until two years before his death, this would mean that the task was spread over an amazing *thirty-three years*!

This theory contradicts the traditional view of when

Nostradamus' prophetic gift developed, suggested by the events of his life. Stories of his second sight did not begin to emerge publicly until he was in his thirties, after the death of his first wife and two children from plague, when it appeared as though the shock of grief might have ignited a dormant prophetic flame that pursued him for the rest of his life.

After he married for the second time in 1547, and settled at Salon in Provence, Nostradamus, now semi-retired as a doctor, turned to writing. From 1550 onwards, he published an annual almanac which was so successful that, in 1555, he brought out a book of prophecies destined to become the first section of *Siècles*.

Again, because of this sequence of events, it has always looked as if he only began writing his prophecies after 1550. But in the secret date concealed in the new title of his prophecies 'The Centuries – His Key – 1531' we have a startling piece of information – that he had begun writing down his prophecies nineteen years earlier than 1550.

This evidence points to the conclusion that the 942 prophecies contained in *Siècles* took him thirty-three years to set down because they were actually not prophecies at all, but coded devices, each one capable of generating a huge amount of information about the future. The reason why Nostradamus would have taken over three decades to write down his work – for most of that period in total secrecy – was that he was not writing prophecies at all, but coded devices disguised as distorted prophecies. What he was really constructing was, as I have said in Chapter One, a kind of instruction programme for later generations to follow. Using the System teaches the brain to detect predictions within the prophetic material. In turn, applying this process over and over again teaches ever more numerous refinements of the System back to the brain. It is the chicken-and-the-egg syndrome with a vengeance, for time, as we understand it to be, is completely eliminated from this process.

The pattern of Nostradamus' earlier life also supports this theory.

Born in 1503 of a family of Jews converted to Roman Catholicism, the young Michel de Nostredame (Nostradamus was his Latinised pen-name) attended the University of Avignon from

Provence – abandoned farm amidst sunflowers and lavender

his early teens. Avignon possessed a large library, including occult works. Here Michel may have come across copies of centuries-old books offering instruction on techniques of concentrating the mind in order to see into the future. There were such works in existence at the end of the Roman Empire and some of them were printed and published during his lifetime.

Some years later, he was discovered teaching his fellow students that the earth was round and that it revolved around the sun. This was a century before Galileo was persecuted by Rome for advancing the same theory. It could be argued that Michel had begun to use these mind-stimulating techniques to good effect, although it is equally possible that, as a brilliant astronomy student, he might

Early telescope in the Greenwich Observatory, London

PROSPECTUS INTRA CAMERAM STELLATAM.

have worked the whole thing out for himself. A further possibility is that he saw a very early paper on the subject by Copernicus who was not to publish his famous work on the subject until 1543. Whatever the reason, Michel had placed himself in danger.

The Church was later to act against Galileo because, as a by-product of his theory, he showed ordinary people the practical means through the use of the telescope whereby the Christian view of the universe, that the earth was its centre and that everything else revolved around it, was proved to be wrong.

Certainly, abstruse papers on these and other controversial theories were circulated to academics in the Church, but they and the universities kept the subject closed to the vast mass of the people, just as political establishments tend to do the same thing today, on the grounds that lack of access to information keeps the people divided, subservient and, above all, quiet.

Nevertheless, we now know that early civilisations, from the Neolithic stone masons to the Ancient Egyptians, were profoundly knowledgeable about astronomy. This knowledge probably never did die out completely, but went underground, to be retained by specialists who needed it for practical purposes. Seamen in the Middle Ages did not need to be told by anyone that the earth was round, least of all by university professors who had never put to sea in their lives. Sailors *knew* the earth was round. For thousands of years they had had the repeated experience of seeing other ships disappearing daily below the horizon.

However, Michel's situation was different in one crucial respect. He was a youth of Jewish descent, whose family's 'devotion' to Roman Catholicism had, like many Jewish families in France, come about after a decree exiling all unconverted Jews from France. It was dangerous for him to be seen spreading ideas that contradicted the Church's teaching in such a fundamental area. His father withdrew him from Avignon and sent him to the renowned medical school at Montpellier, where he obtained his degree within three years.

After some years of great success as an independent practitioner, he returned to Montpellier in 1529 to take his doctorate and then taught there for two years before leaving again, this time for good. So why did he come to abandon a career that should have brought him personal satisfaction and academic honours? It was not because, as an acknowledged brilliant physician, he often found the orthodox methods of treatment inadequate, nor did the reason lie in the fact that he had difficulty coping with the jealousy of colleagues at his success, although both factors might have played a part.

For a person of his character and talent, there could be only one choice. He had decided that he could no longer deny the urgings of a tremendous prophetic gift which he had secretly possessed since birth. Any occult techniques he had acquired along the way had only stimulated that talent, they did not give birth to it.

With his departure from Montpellier in 1531 Michel abandoned all the formal honours which might have been accorded him had he remained, because he had taken a decision which he probably never fully communicated to anyone else for as long as he lived – to write down a huge work of prophecy as his legacy to future generations; in particular, to the generation waiting to cross the divide into the next millennium.

We are that generation.

Decades before his twisted verses were first published, he had begun fashioning them. Previously, his raging talent had probably been sublimated to his medical work and to the natural fear and reluctance which, as a young man, he would have experienced on realising that destiny had picked him out for a dangerous course. He might well have put off the decision for several years, either until he could no longer bear the urge to prophesy, the flame burning ever more strongly with the passing years, or until he had reached a stag where he felt he could both earn a living by practising independent medicine and at the same time be free to begin writing down his prophecies. The known circumstances of his life suggest a personal, intense crisis which the dating code suggests was resolved in 1531.

s	$18 = 9$	$9 + 4 = 13$
Siècles = sien clé	$13 = 4$	$9 - 4 = 5$
		135

This equation reveals the second device in *Siècles*. Verse I.35 was the first of the *Siècles* prophecies to be fulfilled. It was published in 1555 and it came true in 1559. It appeared to foretell harm to the then King of France, Henry II. Henry's queen, Catherine de Medici, alarmed by a similar warning from another astrologer, summoned Nostradamus to Paris in 1556 to interpret the prophecy more fully.

The details describe the death of Henry II in a tournament in Paris in 1559, one of the few public confirmations Nostradamus received during his lifetime that his prophecies were not only accurate but that they were going to capture the imagination of succeeding generations – always, of course, a large part of his purpose. He had to know that his verses would enchant their readers, because by doing so they would survive. Up until the last decade of this millennium, survival has always been the name of the game, as far as Nostradamus was concerned.

What the second part of this *Siècles* device tells us is that, as early as 1531, Nostradamus already knew the number of the first of his prophecies to be fulfilled, perhaps already had a complete plan for the layout of *Siècles* in his mind.

Finally, a point worth making is that the number 94 also appears in this device.

$$18 = 9 \qquad 13 = 4 \qquad 94$$

This book has been published in 1994. This might seem to be a point too far – except for the fact that the year 94 is again confirmed by a prophecy later on in this chapter. Was Nostradamus looking far ahead to the distant decade when the true nature of his prophecies would begin to emerge? It seems so.

What are we to make of this marvellous device which he gave us as the title of his work? As with everything else, it is not just the single detail which convinces, but the cumulative effect of evidence piled upon evidence, confirmation upon confirmation, that reveals to us a phenomenon, the like of which this civilisation has not seen before.

We can seek out more proof in the style of the new predictions offered in this book.

Firstly, there is the swift, dramatic transition from verse prophecy to prose prediction, from muddle to clarity, from mystery to revelation. This transformation is at once so instantaneous and natural that its significance could pass the reader by. There is a very old tradition that Nostradamus wrote down his original prophecies in prose before encapsulating them in the distorted quatrains we know today. It was even believed that a copy of the originals had been hidden with him in his coffin. We know now that this act was never necessary. The prose predictions of future ages have been concealed within his verses from the beginning.

Then there is the fact that when these new predictions emerge from decoding, they mainly use the present tense.

In his original verse prophecies, Nostradamus nearly always uses the future tense or past participles. One of his reasons would have been purely practical. French future or past verb forms employ far more letters than do verbs in the present tense. With the secret predictions using the present tense possessing correspondingly fewer letters, the remaining letters are 'set free' for use in further pieces of coding.

Another reason for the change to the present tense is that when we read these new predictions – vividly and crisply written as though the events they describe were taking place at that precise moment – we share in the spontaneous vision of Nostradamus, the eternal 'Now' to which he constantly had access.

Lastly, the style of writing is exactly the same as in the distorted verse prophecies. In the new prose predictions, it is just more clearly displayed for all to see, loosing a flood of dramatic, informative images combined with a precise insight, a scalpel of language, into each situation described. Irony is used to refer to human folly, but strong compassion reinforces the impact of tragic predictions. An eternal prophetic voice, or the personality of Nostradamus himself? Who, ultimately, can tell?

Having discussed the title and style of the 'new' *Siècles* I turn now to a quatrain which has always been quoted by other interpreters down the centuries as evidence that one day the puzzling verses of Nostradamus would be completely revealed and understood.

De cinq cens ans plus compte l'on tiendra
Celuy qu'estoit l'ornement de son temps,
Puis à un coup grande clarté donra,
Que par ce siècle les rendra tres contens.

III.94

"*For five hundred years more, an accounting will hold fast that which is the ornament of its time. Then at a stroke great clarity will give that which through the century will make them very content.*"

It is immediately obvious that the traditional association of this verse with the prophecies of Nostradamus may be nothing more than wishful thinking. Although it is often said to predict the true revelation of his prophecies, nowhere does there appear to be any evidence even linking it to him, let alone pointing to a new understanding of his predictions!

However, if we apply the methods of decoding explained in this book, the verse suddenly becomes a prose statement that gives us the connective evidence we require.

    a   '   *y*   *i*

De cinq cents ans plus long compte tiendra celui qu'est tôt

               v   *r*

l'ornement de son temps. Puis à un coup grande clarté, donc par

           s

Siècles que rend le race très content.

Note: The use of the apostrophe as a substitute in *long* is a rare feature of the code. The letter g has no numerical value.

For five hundred years the long accounting will hold fast that which is soon the ornament of its time. Then at a stroke great clarity through Siècles *making the race very content.*"

The 'long accounting' refers both to the decades-long construction of *Siècles*, based as it is on a numerical system, and to the centuries when many tried to gain access to the secrets of what was nothing more than a cleverly designed ornament — like a fascinating locket concealing a message within it, or an antique bureau containing numerous secret drawers and compartments. Then, suddenly, without warning, the message will be clear. The locket will be unfastened, the secret compartments will swing open to reveal their contents. Once this has happened it will bring great contentment and peace to the human race.

True to its own self, the prophecy tells us when this great revelation will take place:

a	y	i	v	r	s
t	i	t	u	c	t
1	23	1:9	21	17	18
19	1:9	19	20	3	19
1	5	19	3	8	9
19	19	19	2	3	19
			Mar	8	199
191	195	1991	2	Mar	

The meaning of the dating display is:

"*In 1991, the centuries-old secret of the prophecies will start to be revealed and go on until 1995. By 2–8 March 1999 knowledge of this revelation will be planet-wide, giving inspiration to the human race as it journeys hopefully into the next millennium.*"

In 1991, I published the first fifty predictions of the future using this System. So the first part of this long-hidden prophecy has been now 'activated' by time itself.

The riddle of the phrase 'five hundred years' has often been debated. Nostradamus published the first set of prophecies under the title *Siècles* in 1555. Add on another five hundred years and this would make the date of the revelation 2055, at the earliest.

The true solution is to understand that the phrase *cinq cens ans* does not mean five centuries, but *five hundred-years*, or year numbers which end in a hundred. In other words, Nostradamus is talking about the year at the beginning of each century. If we then start with 1500, the beginning of the century in which he was born, we can select this sequence:

$$1500 \qquad 1600 \qquad 1700 \qquad 1800 \qquad 1900$$

These are the five 'hundred-years' of the riddle.

They are cleverly used in a device to denote when the prophecies will be recognised as an instrument designed to manage society more efficiently for the happiness of all.

First, you add the numbers of the century years above.

$$15 + 16 + 17 + 18 + 19 = 85$$

Then add the numbers of the prophecy 3.94 to 85.

$$85 + 3 + 9 + 4 + 101 \text{ or } 2001$$

By 2001, the equation is saying, the prophecies will have broken out of their time-capsule and be recognised for what they are – devices capable of predicting our future to an ever-expanding degree.

Confirmation of the actual period when this begins to happen is also to be found in the prophecy III.94. It is located close to the year 200.

$$\text{III.94} \qquad\qquad 94 - \text{III} = 91$$
$$1994 \qquad\qquad\qquad 1991$$

The 'great clarity' prophesied by Nostradamus begins to shine through *Siècles* in 1991 – the year when the first book of predictions based on my research was published (*Nostradamus – The End of the Millennium*). Many of these predictions have been fulfilled, or are in the process of coming true.

If we are living in the midst of this great revelation predicted by Nostradamus, it is, he assures us, an experience that will make the human race spiritually content, as we look forward, with his far-sighted help, to meeting all the challenge and excitement of a new age.

CHAPTER 4:

UNDERSTANDING THE CODE

NONE of the modern predictions in this book exists outside the decoding process. You will find them nowhere else. Moreover, none bears the slightest resemblance to the original sixteenth-century prophecy from which it is drawn. To put it another way, their only material form occurs here and the process outlined in this book ensures that they have been 'constructed', rather than written or created. The two guiding principles which I follow are:

a strict adherence to the rules of the decoding system; an explanation of the system appears in the following pages.

the extraction of the maximum amount of meaning within the confines of the system.

This accounts for the unorthodox French in which the predictions are sometimes couched. My intention is always to produce as much meaning as possible, while still linking every letter of the original prophecy through the system to every letter of the new prediction. A prediction full of the most exquisite phrases might *look* pretty, but there would be very few letters remaining from the original prophecy to convey an informative prediction. Placing this aspect of language in its true context, when I began investigating the use of the system thirteen years ago, the predictions that appeared, then and for several years after, were only as long as a single line in a prophetic verse and were almost entirely phonetic. There can be no comparison between those first primitive attempts to master this prophetic mystery and the subtle, detailed predictions which appear in this book.

The dating table which is attached to each prediction, although seeming to possess separate, natural sequences of calculations, should, in my opinion, be treated as a single entity arising from

Michele de Nostradame

the prediction. The dates themselves should be viewed as rising from and falling back into a 'sea' of time; study will reveal that I have by no means, selected all the dates in each table and my research has shown that there are numerous other ways of calculating additional dates than the one I have chosen.

I am not a natural seer. I do not possess the gift of prophecy. For information about the future, I have to rely solely on the system of decoding which I have established through investigation of the texts over the last thirteen years. As I have grown wiser in the art of using this marvellous, flexible system, the predictions have grown ever more complex and subtle in their use of language. Nevertheless, the principles of the system remain paramount. The system is my pole star guiding me through uncharted waters. I regard it as sacrosanct, in command of every aspect of this strange process – French prediction, English translation, dating and interpretation. When each prediction emerges from the process, every one of its letters is linked, either directly, or indirectly, to the original prophecy from which it is drawn. Without this overriding principle, I would find myself adrift, directionless among the mists of the future.

The idea behind the method of detection which I use is that all of Nostradamus' prophetic verses are really devices – carefully assembled sets of letters – which can produce predictions using Seven Rules.

The system, correctly and constantly used, actually 'teaches' the eye and brain to recognise predictions. The prophetic devices themselves contain a programme of detailed information about the future.

Each original prophecy can produce predictions 'to order' by extracting the letters of the subject which an interpreter wants to know about, followed by the extraction of the dating code chosen to 'access' this information.

The remaining letters of the prophecy are an anagram. Solve the anagram and a prediction emerges about the chosen subject. Follow the rules exactly and that prediction will be accurate.

I have established the validity of these rules over many years of research. They control the direction of the prediction and prevent it from whizzing off in some unlikely or nonsensical direction.

All the predictions in this book have been decoded from the list of prophetic quatrains following this explanation.

These are the basic rules:

Rule One   Decide on the subject on which prophetic information is required.

Rule Two   Extract the letters of the subject from a prophetic quatrain.

Rule Three   Extract the letters of the dating code chosen.

The prophetic quatrains were never intended by Nostradamus to be fully revealed until 1991 when, using the new System, fifty predictions for 1991–2001 were published. This decade before the millennium is therefore to be regarded as an 'introductory' approach to a complete prophetic revelation.

To produce long-term predictions from 1995 I have chosen the code word *cinq* or 'five'. Each predicted year up to 1999 has its own date code. That is to say, if I had chosen to begin this period in 1996, I would have begun each relevant prediction with the code word *six*. My theory is that these date codes ensure that the prediction emerges out of the desired period of time.

If I were, however, using the prophecy to detect a description of what, to us, is a prophecy of the past, say, the battle of Waterloo, I would not need a date code. A reference to the 'battle of Waterloo' would suffice, since there is no other famous battle in history known by that name. This is not possible with detecting predictions of the future — before 1815, we would have had to know about the battle of Waterloo in order to detect a prophecy about the battle of Waterloo, if you see what I mean!

The period 2000 onwards is signified by the phrase *après l'an deux mille* or 'after the year two thousand'.

In a few prophecies, I have not used either of these dating codes. This is because they were decoded in 1991, a year which was a watershed in history for the understanding of the prophecies. No predictions decoded in that year needed such a date code.

I have tried to select dates that occur within the period stated. However, some dates may fall before or after the period — this is because the future, just like history, will not confine the impact of its events to a particular period just because we want to dissect a slice of it.

Readers may sometimes quarrel with my choice of dates, but unless that reader is Nostradamus reborn one interpretation is as valid as another. It may turn out that the System is so constructed that *whatever* dates are selected, they will be relevant to the prediction. Each set of dates embedded in the text of a particular prediction may not be allowed to stray out of a well defined 'corridor of time'.

One final, very important point. The date codes are expressed in text, because the text dictates the direction of the prediction. *Although dating is important, it is secondary to the correct decoding of the text. Only when that is complete, should the dating system be invoked. They are always two quite separate activities.*

Rule 4   All the letters in the original prophecy must be used up. Otherwise, the prediction will not be accurate and the dating system will be affected.

Rule 5   If it is required, a 'new' letter may be substituted for an 'old' letter from the original prophecy. 'Old' and 'new' letters are always shown together, old immediately above the new. Normally, only one letter per word may be substituted in this way. (See *Exceptions* below).

	s
Example: *Siècles*	*sien clé*
Centuries	his key

For an explanation of this phrase, you should turn to Chapter 3.

Both sets of letters then go on to justify their place in the text by combining to form the Dating System.

Rule 6   Each 'old' and 'new' letter has its own number. These numbers combine to form a dating display producing years, months and days connected with the new prediction.

| s | | s | | 18 | 9 |
| *Siècles* | | *sien clé* | | n | 13 | 4 |

The Numerical Alphabet is made up of 24 letters/numbers.

a	**b**	**c**	**d**	**e**	**f**	**g**	**h**	**i**	**j**	**l**	**m**
1	2	3	4	5	6	7	8	1:9	10	11	12
n	**o**	**p**	**q**	**r**	**s**	**t**	**u**	**v**	**x**	**y**	**z**
13	14	15	16	17	18	19	20	21	22	23	24

Note that the letter 'i' has two numbers 1 and 9. This is because I is also the Roman numeral 'One'. The letters V and X are also 5 and 10 for the same reason, but are used less frequently.

When using the dating system, 19 can be reduced to 10 or 1, and 1 can grow to 19 by the same process:

$$1 = 10 = 1:9 = 19 = 1:9 = 10 = 1$$

Zero can be added or deducted from a number, i.e. 20 becomes 2, or 3 becomes 30. (For further information, see *Exceptions* below).

Rule 7

Only the letters above the text ('old' letters from the prophecy) and the 'new' letters they surmount are used in the Dating System.

The dating display in this book is produced in three lines.

The numbers relating to the letters themselves are displayed.

In the second line, single-digit numbers remain the same. If a number contains two digits these are added together. Example: 14 cannot be a month of the year, but added together it becomes 5 or May.

Numbers not added together are 19 when the Dating System is indicating a period before 2000 and 20 when it applies to after 2000. Where 20 does not occur, but 2 does, then the code may also understand this to be after 2000.

In all attempts to analyse the Dating System, the interpreter must be guided by the sense and direction of the prediction already decoded, as well as referring to other predictions relating to the same subject or period.

Study of the Dating System soon makes it clear that the it is split up into little 'clocks' of dates which run either clockwise or anti clockwise. Year dates occur such as 97 or 197 (1997) and 204 (2004) followed by the day and the month.

The combinations 19:19, 19:10, 10:19 and 10:10, as well as 10 by itself, signify the year 2000. The combinations 2 or 20, plus 1:9, 19, or 10 signify 2010.

These are the ground rules which I have found to be most useful in detecting the dates of predictions. The system has other refinements, but they are not referred to in this book.

Exceptions to
Rules Five and Six

Two letters are missing from the 24-letter alphabet – k and w. *This means that, although they may occur in a prediction, they are not used to calculate dates.*

When k needs to appear in the new prediction, it must have a substitute or 'old' letter from the original prophecy displayed above it. This letter will, of course, have a number which is used in the dating system.

Letter from the original prophecy	*a*	*l*
New Letter	*k*	—

Occasionally, *k* appears in an original prophecy itself, such as III.53 in the following Appendix. When this happens, it may be used in a word where it appears normally, such as in the name 'Mikhail Gorbachev'.

With the letter *w*, the actual sound is 'double-u', so naturally two *u*'s are the substitute for *w* in the text.

uu

William

Both *w* and 2 *u*'s used in this way do not possess numbers of their own, so no dating attaches to them.

Text	Value
uu	—
w	—

It follows that when *w* is present in the new prediction, a double letter substitution may be made. This is the only exception to the rule (as far as I have established) that one letter only per word may be substituted. (For a suitable example of substitution involving both *w* and *k* see 'Stephen Hawking Explains the Universe'.

Appendix

THE new predictions in this book have all been decoded from the following original verse prophecies of Nostradamus appearing in his work *Siècles* or 'Centuries'.

Note that in certain cases I have added the natural letter to the line, while placing the old letter above. Such letters were always a visible clue to the deciphering of the prophecies.

I. 28

La tour de Boucq craindra fuste barbare
v
Un temps longtemps apres barque hesperique,
Bestail ges, meubles, tous deux ferot grad tare,
Taurius et Libra, quell mortelle picque. Prophecy

I. 35

   y i
Le lion jeune le vieux surmontera,
En champ bellique par singulier duelle,
      y u
Dans cage d'or les yeux lui crevera,
  v
Deux classes une puis mourir mort cruelle.

I. 42   u

Le dix Calende d'Avril de faict Gotique,
Resuscité encor par gens malins,
Le feu estainct, assemble diabolique,
Cherchant les os du d'Amant et Pielin

II. 51   i

Le sang de juste à Londres fera faute,
Bruslez par foudres de vingt trois les six,
La dame antique cherra de place haute,
De mesme secte plusieurs seront occis.

III. 53

Quand le plus grand emportera le pris
De Nuremberg, d'Ausbourg, et ceux de Basle,
Par Ahrippine chef Frankfort repris,
         i
Trauerferont per Flamant jusqu'en Gale.

III. 65   n
Quand le sepulchre du grand Romain trouvé
  i
Le jour après sera esleu Pontife
           u
Du Senat gueres il ne sera prouvé,
Empoisonné, son sang au sacré scyphe

LES
PROPHETIES
DE M. MICHEL
NOSTRADAMVS.

Centuries VIII. IX. X.

Qui n'ont encores iamais esté imprimees.

A LYON,
PAR BENOIST RIGAVD.

Title page of the original edition of *Les Propheties*

IV. 44

Deux gros de Mende, et de Roudés et Milhau
Cahours, Limoges, Castres malo sepmano,
                      v
De nuech l'intrado, de Bourdeaux un cailhau,
Par Perigort au toc de la campano. Prophecy

VII. 14

Faux exposer viendra topographie,
                          u
Seront les cruches de monuments ouvertes,
Pulluler secte, faincte philosophie,
Pour blanches, noires, et pour antiques vertes.

VII. 4

Dedans Monech le coq fera receu
Le Cardinal de France apparoistra,
Par Logarion Romain fera deceu
Foiblesse à l'Aigle, et force au Coq naistra.

IX. 36

 v   **v** **i**
Un grand Roy prins entre le mains d'un jeune
Non loin de Pasques, confusion, coup cultre,
Perpet. captif temps que foudre en la hune
Trois freres lors se blesseront, et murtre.

X. 89

De brique en marbre feront les murs reduicts,
Sept et cinquante années pacifique,
Ioye aux humains, renoue l'aqueduict,
Sante, grands fruicts, ioye et temps melifique.

Acknowledgements

My thanks to Elspeth Lindner, who originally commissioned this book; to my editors Sarah Hannigan and Emma Rhind-Tutt at Heinemann for much time and work spent on its production; to Susan Rose-Smith for tackling so well the daunting picture research. I give special thanks to my agent, Rosemary Canter. To all members, past and present, of the Quill Club, thank you for keeping up my interest in writing over the years. Always, my deep gratitude goes to Derek, Jeremy, Ian and Alan for putting up with my pet obsession.

Credits

Numbers refer to pages on which pictures occur:
J Allen Cash 20, 74; Associated Press/Topham 177; Ian Berry/Magnum 249; Bridgeman 19, 23, 245; British Library (MPL) 246; Rene Burri/Magnum 238; Camera Press 30, 34, 42, 154, 195, 230, 231; JL Charmet 2, 3, 4, 16; Comstock 128, 200, 237; Sue Cunningham 220, 224, 225; Fotomas 272, 312; Tim Graham 49, 51, 52, 55, 79; Grumman Aircraft Systems Group 119, 257; Erich Hartmann/Magnum 110; Geoff Howard 64, 84, 89, 91, 104, 130, 170, 226; Hulton-Deutsch Collection 82, 102, 275; Image Bank 45, 92, 131, 188, 198, 208; AF Kersting 133; Keystone/Sygma 137; Frank Lane 277; Los Alamos National Library/SPL 283; Magnum 126, 185, 203, 233, 234, 294; Barney Magrath/Science Photo Library 269; Peter Menzel/Science Photo Library 107, 268; Tony Morrison South American Pictures 242; MPL 155, 205, 210, 288, 295; NASA/Science Photo Library 252, 265; David Parker/SPL 180; Picturepoint 60, 97, 280; Popperfoto 215; Rex 24, 33, 63, 66, 117, 121, 142 (1 & 2), 145, 148, 156, 160, 172, 218; Eddie Ryle-Hodges 69, 72; Scala 33; Ronald Sheridan 122, 258, 304; Edwin Smith 77; SPL 192, 193, 255; Sygma 87, 98, 139, 142 (3), 174, 187, 219; Topham 36, 39, 40, 56, 114, 115, 150, 152, 161, 162, 165, 167, 168, 214; US Geological Survey / Science Photo Library 262.